Key West Gardens and their Stories

Key West Gardens and their Stories

JANIS FRAWLEY-HOLLER

Photographs by Darrel F. Holler

 PINEAPPLE PRESS, INC.
Sarasota, Florida

ACKNOWLEDGMENTS

The seed for the book was planted by Carol Wightman, owner/manager of the Marquesa Hotel, who, when her garden was honored with a prestigious award, suggested I write an article about the gardens of Key West. Pam Davidson, my friend since grade school, encouraged me to expand the article into a book.

Carol introduced me to her landscape architect, Raymond Jungles, who showed me his other masterpieces, and to landscape artist Patrick Tierney, who took me on a tour of not only the gorgeous gardens he has designed but others throughout the island. His contacts, help, and encouragement proved invaluable to me.

From there it was word of mouth, with Craig Reynolds, Raymond's associate landscape architect, extending his talent, Nancy Forrester steering me yet to other gardens, Kittie Clements opening doors to secret places, Trip Hoffman adding even more diversity, Christopher Cowen contributing his flair, and Kenneth Weschler offering gardens he keeps in tip-top shape. Special thanks to June and David Cussen of Pineapple Press, who reified the dream of writing this book; to Kris Rowland, who was a joy to work with; and to Carol Tornatore for her fabulous design.

Other people have contributed in so many different ways: my father, James, who told me to follow my heart; my mother, Frances, who inspired stick-to-itiveness; my sister, Jacklyn Treneer, who offered support and encouragement; and my niece, Chrystal, who has a "writer" within. My master-gardener friend, Andrea Griggs, never tired of my questions or my borrowing her books; good friend Gabrielle Guilmette helped with her insight; and my friend since college, Celeste Nottingham, came to Key West from Colorado with a heart full of support and pride.

I extend a loving thank you to Darrel Holler, my husband, photographer, greatest source of support, and best friend.

Except during specified garden tours, please respect the privacy of those people who have so graciously shared the beauty of their gardens with us in this book. See the Foreword for tour information.

Inquiries should be addressed to:

Pineapple Press, Inc.
P.O. Box 3899
Sarasota, Florida 34230

www.pineapplepress.com.

Library of Congress Cataloging in Publication Data

Frawley-Holler, Janis
    Key West gardens and their stories / Janis Frawley-Holler ; photographs by Darrel F. Holler.—1st ed.
        p.   cm.
    ISBN 1-56164-204-5 (pbk. : alk. paper)
    1. Gardens—United States—Key West. 2. Gardens—United States—Key West—Pictorial works. I. Title.

SB466.U65 K484 2000
712'.09759'41—dc21

                                                                            00-031358

First Edition
10 9 8 7 6 5 4 3 2

Design by Carol Tornatore Creative Design
Printed in China

For my father, who guided me from beyond,
and my mother, who encouraged me
with all her heart

Contents

Introduction

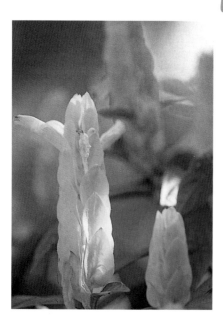

Key West is an island paradise of tropical gardens. They are hidden behind ginger-bread-trimmed homes built by early shipbuilders, wrapped around new houses sitting on a site rich in naval history, and line narrow front yards of cottages where nineteenth-century Cuban cigar rollers once lived. And many are tucked away beyond the dead ends of secret alleys.

These gardens are magical, romantic and epitomize carefree living in a place where the sun's heat slows the pace of human life but rallies the souls of tropical plants from all over the world. The trade winds blow away the pressures of daily living yet give birth to the flora by spreading their pollen and seeds. And the welcome rain cools the temperature, adding to the energy of life as it nourishes the plants of all the island yards.

The rhythm of life here is more Caribbean than American. And so is the cadence of its gardens, thanks to the warming influence of the nearby Gulf Stream, which makes Key West a frost-free, tropical island in every sense except latitude.

Originally, houses were built on small, narrow lots with little room for front and side yards. Back yards were deep to accommodate cookhouses, vegetable gardens, and cisterns that caught and stored valued rainwater. Seafaring men returned from voyages throughout the Caribbean and South America with seedlings of tropical fruit trees, such as sugar apples and sapodillas, as gifts for their wives, who made scrumptious jellies, ice creams, and marinades from the fruits of more southerly ports. These trees still thrive.

By the mid-1930s, gardening had become meaningful enough that Miss Jessie Porter organized the island's first flower show. All came carrying their best blooms to a World War I warehouse in the Navy yard. She handpicked an impressive trio of judges: Ernest Hemingway, John Dos Passos, and writer/adventurer George Allen England. To ensure the success of the event, Miss Jessie whipped up a huge batch of strong, fruity rum punch. The judges imbibed so much, and had so much fun, that they awarded every entry in the show first-prize ribbons . . . until the ribbons ran out.

You will feel that same heady intoxication as you discover the magic of so many Key West gardens that flourish on this tiny island blessed by the warmth of the Gulf Stream.

VISITING PRIVATE GARDENS

This book offers the only public view of some of the gardens featured here. You are requested to honor privacy. However, there are several annual opportunities to peek behind the white picket fences and view private gardens in Key West. The Old Island Restoration Foundation presents its Annual House & Garden Tours, a series of five tours each featuring five or six homes and their gardens, starting with the evening Holiday Tour during Christmas week. Then there is a tour in January, one in February, and two tours in March. Proceeds benefit restoration of the island's historical homes and landmarks. Information: 305-294-9501.

Every March the Key West Garden Club alternates its Garden Tours of up to six private gardens with its impressive, accredited Standard Flower Show, based on themes such as "Where the Tropics Begin." Proceeds help to maintain the historic West Martello Tower, the Club's beautiful home. Information: 305-294-3210.

For ease of reading and identification, the common names of plants and flowers are used throughout the book; scientific names are cited when no known alternative is available.

Restful Respites Open to All

NANCY FORRESTER'S SECRET GARDEN

"Such sights as youthful poets dream . . ."

—*John Milton*

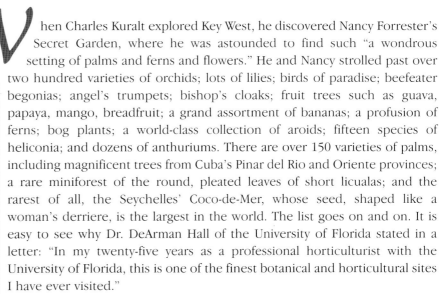

When Charles Kuralt explored Key West, he discovered Nancy Forrester's Secret Garden, where he was astounded to find such "a wondrous setting of palms and ferns and flowers." He and Nancy strolled past over two hundred varieties of orchids; lots of lilies; birds of paradise; beefeater begonias; angel's trumpets; bishop's cloaks; fruit trees such as guava, papaya, mango, breadfruit; a grand assortment of bananas; a profusion of ferns; bog plants; a world-class collection of aroids; fifteen species of heliconia; and dozens of anthuriums. There are over 150 varieties of palms, including magnificent trees from Cuba's Pinar del Rio and Oriente provinces; a rare miniforest of the round, pleated leaves of short licualas; and the rarest of all, the Seychelles' Coco-de-Mer, whose seed, shaped like a woman's derriere, is the largest in the world. The list goes on and on. It is easy to see why Dr. DeArman Hall of the University of Florida stated in a letter: "In my twenty-five years as a professional horticulturist with the University of Florida, this is one of the finest botanical and horticultural sites I have ever visited."

When I rang the ship's bell and entered the gate to this garden of Eden, I allowed myself to stand still, to take a deep breath of the natural perfumes in the air, and to listen to the tropical breeze arousing the leaves of a canopy so high it can be seen from the harbor. Soon the junglelike calls of parrots

11

and macaws echoed throughout, and Nancy appeared, exuding the soul of Mother Earth—a green thumb to match—and knowledgeable enough to lecture in prestigious places like Miami's Fairchild Tropical Garden. She rescued this acre, where hundred-year-old Caribbean fruit trees have grown since seamen planted them. It was actually an undesignated dump, which the city finally condemned and was going to do a clean sweep of, including the venerable trees.

"When we started digging, shards of other people's lives showed up," Nancy said, "from good China from England to antique glass to clay marbles, which occasionally still appear. Then on Sunday afternoons, when people were doing yard work, I went around, collected cuttings, planted them, and received great joy out of watching them grow."

Then her cousin Peter Whelan's passion for rare palms infected her, and over the years her garden evolved into what brides think of as a most beautiful spot to say "I do."

"Mine is a garden filled with blessings and vows," Nancy said, referring to the hundreds of marriages performed here. Wedding stories abound, including the one of a woman who arranged a grand ceremony to marry herself, vowing to always treat herself with kindness and respect, then threw a slumber party in the rental garden cottage. One couple released butterflies; another was serenaded with bagpipes and dulcimers. Stranger requests come too, like the one from a woman who had hunted the globe for a birthing circle and found it right here. Then there was the lady who danced the tango in the garden, teary-eyed, as Nancy listened to her tragic love story.

Each who walks here falls under the garden's spell in his own way. All are amazed that this masterpiece of natural art grows at the end of a secret alley in Old Town.

LOCATION: **One Free School Lane**

THE HYATT KEY WEST'S TURTLE GARDEN

"Wisely and slow; they stumble that run fast."

—Shakespeare

I love the "turtle garden" at the Hyatt Resort and so does everyone else. It's a fun spot, cool and shady in the embrace of areca palms, colorful bromeliads, and the twirling form of a gorgeous screw pine, named for the spiral pattern of its leaves. Orchids are suspended in wooden baskets from its branches above a pond teeming with resident turtles.

The "star" of the group slowly makes his way out of the water and up the ramp that leads to a tiny sandy beach built to inspire egg-laying. He ignores the little sign that reads "No Diving," dodges a white phaleanopsis orchid, and inches his way to the sand's rocky edge. Some hang out beneath waterfalls, whose rushing flow adds to the magic, while others just swim around until the sun shines full above. Then all the turtles mosey up a log in single file to sunbathe in a setting lush with bamboo, feathery pygmy date palms, and the huge tropical leaves of white birds of paradise.

This is a delightful little garden guaranteed to bring a smile.

LOCATION: **601 Front Street**

THE MEDICINE GARDEN

"We teach what we need to learn."

—Anonymous

nside the woven bamboo fence that separates the Medicine Garden from the rest of the world is a mystical place where sound is silenced except for a soothing waterfall, the softest of wind chimes, and the occasional coo of a dove. The air is still and healing beneath the spreading canopy of an old mahogany tree, whose immense trunk is masked by jungly philodendron vines. Two royal poinciana trees spread their brilliant red flowers into the treetops.

Beneath, the garden is Merlinesque, with little niches and low walls embedded with masses of thick glass, purple amethyst gemstones, colored glass balls, and gigantic crystals steadfast in a base of seashells, all catching and reflecting the sun's rays. A fat-'n-happy Hoi Toi reigns in a private cubbyhole near a gigantic, night-blooming cereus cactus whose stiff, thick arms stretch upward, blessing the garden with hundreds of ivory flowers at night. Weather-seasoned pieces of Jamaican dogwood sit beside those of the heaviest of all woods, lignum vitae, the "wood of life," both gnarly and sensuously curved by nature, giving the impression of sea-sculpted driftwood.

It is within this Druid-like meditation circle where I met Pejuta, a bare-footed man wearing a beaded ankle bracelet and radiating a monk-like inner peace. This is his garden, and he welcomes anyone seeking quiet space during daylight hours. A transplant from Tennessee who has taken a Native American name meaning "healing roots," Pejuta one day decided to go as far south as he possibly could without leaving the

United States. In 1983, he bought this land of horse stables and took five years to transform it into the most novel garden on the island.

The seating walls and borders of the pathways were hand built, some from the original coral rock foundation of old natives' houses, others from blue slate and granite curbstones the city discarded when it modernized the streets. Now they're etched with geckos, fish, suns, and birds and surrounded with bromeliads, bright crotons, and large green pads of prickly pear cacti dressed in Christmas-red buds.

We walked together along the shaded wooden path to a small koi pond whose back wall holds pink conch shells with water trickling down from their lips. Bunches of bamboo grow around the pool, reflecting the twinkling lights that hover above. Affirmations, such as "Embrace things as they are," are painted in opportune places.

A bamboo, Robinson Crusoe–style tree house lies beyond the koi pond, decorated with Native American artifacts, from antlers to drums to planters and gourd bird feeders. Pejuta's pet albino African frog lives in a private puddle pool. The second-floor deck, where trees grow through the straw-matted floor, gives this gentle man an exceptional view of his garden as well as of the woodpecker family living in the birdhouse that hangs from the high mahogany limbs.

In this garden, group meditations are held two evenings a week by the light of bamboo torches. Throughout the year, guest appearances by leaders of all paths are hosted in the Meditation Circle. So stroll or find a little niche in which to sit and unwind. It's the best "medicine" in the world.

LOCATION: **800 Amelia Street**

THE PALM GARDEN
OF THE LIBRARY

"For the wind is in the palm trees . . ."

—Rudyard Kipling

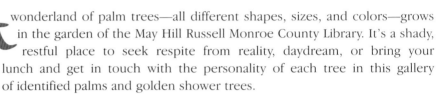

A wonderland of palm trees—all different shapes, sizes, and colors—grows in the garden of the May Hill Russell Monroe County Library. It's a shady, restful place to seek respite from reality, daydream, or bring your lunch and get in touch with the personality of each tree in this gallery of identified palms and golden shower trees.

The maitre d' of the garden is a noble Canary Island date palm. Ancient documents record it as one of the oldest cultivated plants on earth. Nearby is Cuba's old man palm, the most fun of all, clothed in long, dense, golden "hair." The Cuban Baily *copernicia*, one of the world's most magnificent fan palms, has a massive trunk that reaches a strapping width of five feet.

Florida is well represented. Its state tree, the sabal palm, is a pioneer trying to survive over-harvesting in the wild for its tasty "swamp cabbage," known to gourmets as hearts of palm. The saw palmetto, brought here from Lake Okeechobee, is a rarity in that it is 150 years old, is very large, and has ten feet of roots. And the palmlike coontie, actually a prehistoric plant of the cycad family, was used by Seminole Indians to make bread after they washed and kneaded away its poison.

The Florida thatch palm appears carefree in its circular leaves, while the classy silver thatch palm twinkles glittery-white in the sun. An endangered buccaneer palm, the rarest of all Florida natives, boasts blue-green fronds atop a trunk of remarkable stripes. The resilient, seventy-year-old Key thatch palms, rescued after a fire raged through the pinelands, still bear the scars of that blaze. There are also many palms from the world's most enticing ports of call.

Designing this public garden was a dream come true for landscape artist Patrick Tierney. With his expertise in the palms of the world, along with funds so generously donated by Key West/Wisconsin steel industrialist and philanthropist Duane Rath, the community was presented with this quiet refuge, where enchanting palm trees sway in the sea breeze for all to enjoy.

LOCATION: **700 Fleming Street**

THE GARDENS OF ST. PAUL'S EPISCOPAL CHURCH

"... and a garden causes seeds to grow."

—Isaiah 61:11

The gardens of St. Paul's Episcopal Church feel warm and safe, just like a big hug from nature. Maybe it's because of the great age of the church, which stands tall and proud with its historic tenacity rooted in the grounds, or the picture of its grand white steeple stretching high toward the sky, reminiscent of simpler times.

St. Paul's was founded in 1831, when its services were held at the county courthouse in Jackson Square. The first southernmost church was built on land bought for one dollar from the widow of John Fleming. In return, she asked that her husband's grave on the property remain undisturbed. Hence, he lies beneath the church, his gravestone part of an inside wall near the altar.

The church weathered destruction from fire and hurricanes time and again but was always rebuilt. Near the turn of the century, an energetic and artistic rector, Reverend Higgs, planted an ornamental garden so exquisite it was considered the island's showplace. Unfortunately, the 1909 hurricane ravaged both garden and church.

Plantings today boast a simpler beauty that includes a wealth of rosebushes of all colors scattered about in containers. Nowhere on the island is the royal poinciana, the world's most colorful tree, as stunning, its magnificent scarlet flowers contrasting with the gleaming white church. It marks the starting point of the footpath that guides you through the grounds. A statue of St. Francis of Assisi stands beneath overhanging blossoms of a frilly Japanese hibiscus bush. An elderly banyan tree and a nearby spider palm shade the historic rectory. The finale at the end of the walk is St. Paul's Memorial Garden, first planted in the late 1830s and still holding on to the characteristics of an old-fashioned Key West garden.

Thick, purple bougainvillea envelop its fence, and at the front of the grassy oasis, a stage for Easter sunrise services and egg hunts, stand two ancient mahogany trees. Venerable *tabebuia* and autograph trees tower over the statue of a beautiful angel. Worn by time and salt air, she watches over the columbarium. White, outdoor loveseats sit in the shade of the tall trees, a perfect place to spend some quiet reflective time and experience the feel of an earlier island era.

But the most soul-stirring way to experience this comfortable garden is from within the peacefulness of the church. As I walked toward the altar, the sun filtered in through the rich colors of the antique collection of stained-glass windows, some dating back to the 1920s. I slid into a pew near the front, where the lower windows pivot open, allowing the trade winds to carry in the subtle scents of jasmine and frangipani. The verandah outside holds clay pots planted with Mexican heather and roses; beyond is a backdrop of dappled crotons, red caladeums, bundles of bamboo, rich red hibiscus, and ixoras.

It's an experience guaranteed to nurture your spirit.

LOCATION: **401 Duval Street**

THE KEY WEST HISTORIC MEMORIAL SCULPTURE GARDEN

"... many valiant souls of heroes."

—*Homer*

To stroll the Walkway of History in the Key West Historic Memorial Sculpture Garden is to rendezvous with the men and women who have made significant contributions to the evolution of an island so bold and independent it threatened secession from the Union in 1982. The very nature of the Key West spirit is deeply rooted in its "Conchs," the pioneering Loyalist families who sailed to Key West from the Bahamas with hopes of bettering their lives after farming virtually failed on their islands. In the 1800s, they found their dream of riches in wrecking, the salvaging of cargo from ships that had crashed into the reefs off the island. It is these ties to the Bahamas that sparked Ida Barron's idea of a sculpture garden similar to the Loyalist Memorial Sculpture Garden in New Plymouth, Key West's sister city on Green Turtle Cay in the Abaco archipelago. When she was dying of cancer, Ed Swift, president of the Friends of Mallory Square, visited Ida. She confided her dream to Ed, who felt compelled to make his friend's lifelong wish come true.

Award-winning Miami sculptor James Mastin created the haunting emotions of the garden's centerpiece, titled simply *The Wreckers*. This bronze sculpture freezes in time the men who braved foul weather and angry seas to save lives and cargo from broken ships. Their essence is captured in two wreckers on the deck of a crumbling ship who rescue a frightened little girl clinging to her doll while they raise valuable cargo from the hold.

Surrounding *The Wreckers* are the original thirty-six busts of historical figures whose eyes gaze directly and unforgettably into yours and that offer a history lesson as they sit atop coral pedestals fronted with bronze plaques inscribed with their contributions to the island. The famous are here, such as resident Ernest Hemingway and vacationer Harry Truman.

But the most intriguing stories lie with the lesser known, such as Sandy Cornish, a one-time slave who ensured his freedom by inflicting injuries upon himself and whose fruit orchard, frequented by Union soldiers, made him wealthy. Or Sister Gabriel, who turned the island's convent into a hospital to tend the wounded of the Spanish-American War. Or Eduardo Gato, owner of the largest cigar factory on the isle. These are the spirits that remain here amidst flowering hibiscus and Alexandra palms.

The walkway itself is a unique experience, its red bricks etched with quips and quotes. A fund-raiser to ensure perpetual care of the garden, the walkway contains over seventy thousand bricks that will bear names and messages from the world over. You could spend hours reading the inscriptions, which range from the expected Key West humor ("He could have sold seawater to Columbus") to those placed by the Square of Honor for Keys' residents killed during wartime.

Time can get away from you as you immerse yourself in the soul of a garden that confirms Key West's ties to islands farther south.

LOCATION: **Mallory Square**

Gardens with a Past

AUDUBON HOUSE AND TROPICAL GARDENS

"God Almighty planted the first garden.
And, indeed, it is the purest of human pleasures."

—*Francis Bacon*

A stand of Jamaican Tall coconut palms, over one hundred years old, towers over the Audubon House and Tropical Gardens, originally the 1846 estate of Capt. John Geiger. They share the sky with a 150-year-old tropical almond tree, a century-old tamarind tree, and many sapodilla trees well over eighty years of age. This is just a sampling of what the captain would have brought back from his voyages throughout the Caribbean and South America and planted in his yard.

Captain Geiger hosted celebrated naturalist John James Audubon, who painted eighteen of his world-renowned birds of America right on these grounds. Charmed by the orange flowers of the Geiger tree, he used its branches in his paintings of the white-crowned pigeon. He also painted his pipery flycatcher/gray kingbird here on a branch of the hummingbird tree, beset with its unusually shaped reddish-pink flowers. It has since been named the Audubon tree. Both grow near the entrance of the home.

I love plant perusing here with the *Tropical Garden Guide* in hand because it reveals tidbits and tales I wouldn't have known: the Spanish stopper growing beside the outhouse was a pioneer remedy for diarrhea; the king sago is a living fossil, once food for dinosaurs; pirates and early Spaniards used knives to carve symbols and messages on the leaves of the autograph tree and sent them as notes or etched them as decks of playing

cards to pass away time. Today, tourists use the tree at the front corner of the house to commemorate their visit here, which makes for fun reading.

The center of the garden is bricked with islands of plantings. A border of one-hundred-year-old hand-blown bottles, whose colors reflect the sun's rays, frame creeping ficus topiaries of sandhill cranes with frilly, red, Japanese lantern hibiscus bowing overhead. The crimson trunk of a lipstick palm stands out, as do the bromeliads running up the trunk of a coconut palm. One bed hosts a minigrouping of *Licuala grandis* palms with their showy, pleated leaves growing in the shade of a sapodilla, along with bright-pink ti plants. Another overflows in leather ferns with cherry-red spicy jatropha blooming from its center.

The grounds excel in fruit trees and even offer a secret little orchard next to the gift shop. There are Barbados cherries bursting with one thousand times more vitamin C than an orange; guavas, which make delicious jelly and duffs; loquat trees, whose figlike fruit is popular in tropical markets; soursops so prized for marinades that in 1887 locals paid 50 cents a fruit; and Key limes and sugar apples.

A first-class assortment of plantings, rich in color and texture, encircle this historical property: lighthearted yellow turneras, burgundy arecas, the heart-shaped leaves of scarlet glory bowers, purply-pink beauty berries, hedges of wild coffee, giant crinum lilies, and staghorn ferns. Hibiscus and ginger grow in pinks and reds. Huge tropical leaves of banana trees and heliconia sway in the breeze. And orchids (brassavolas, cattleyas, dendrobiums, encyclias, phaleonopsis, vandas, vanillas, and schomburgkias) are just some of the species that thrive attached to tree trunks.

An herb-and-butterfly garden flourishes out back, where an antique gate from Savannah opens onto purple wild petunia, light-pink pentas and periwinkles, scarlet milkweed, and wild cotton. The bees and butterflies are busy back here, so sit in the shadows of the firebush and watch one of nature's best shows.

It is easy to see why this museum was voted the best in Florida by *South Florida* magazine. It is the ultimate combination of the history of a seafaring family, the artistry of Audubon, and the beauty of a famous botanical garden, where, appropriately, all tours of the property begin and end.

LOCATION: **205 Whitehead Street**

24

THE ERNEST HEMINGWAY HOME AND MUSEUM

". . . discover the concealed beauties of a writer."

—Joseph Addison

For writers and readers, the gardens of the Ernest Hemingway Home and Museum mean stepping on hallowed ground. The unique two-story home was built in 1851 by shipping magnate Asa Tift and purchased for eight thousand dollars in 1931 for the Hemingways by Pauline's Uncle Gus. Its arched doorways and floor-to-ceiling windows are dressed in Key lime–green shutters, its verandahs in ornate, black wrought iron. This mix of French Quarter and South Seas plantation styles is as much a focal point of the garden as the uncommon, majestic sandbox tree at the corner of the home. Planted in the '30s by Ernest himself, its trunk towers past the roof of the house and is wonderfully thick, gnarled, and covered in ferocious thorns that keep wildlife at bay, including the famous six-toed cats that live here. A native of the West Indies, its dried berries were turned into sand, which was used to dry ink.

Pauline planted the pothos philodendron vines, which have crawled their way into the sandbox tree's canopy, their leaves growing larger the higher they go. Then, as if on a whim, they hang downward, suspended and swaying in the wind. The tree sits in an ocean of ferns, magenta ti plants, and Bismarck palms, showing off their silvery, starry leaves.

The garden path continues to offer a wide variety of plants, such as tropical gingers, fields of large-leafed elephant ears, and a section of antique Spanish tiles Ernest brought back from Cuba's Presidential Palace. Barbados cherry trees host orchids. Papaya and banana trees bear fruit, and Key limes furnished the juice for the Hemingways' daiquiris. Off in a secret corner is a little cemetery where the cats are buried, their headstones engraved with names like Kim Novak and Spencer Tracy.

At the base of the stairs to Papa's writing studio is Pauline's garden, shaded by bamboo with pots from Spain that hold tri-colored dracaenas. A Cuban olive jar, enveloped in yellow-trunked bamboo and the incredible walking roots of a huge screw pine, doubles as a fountain. Water quietly runs down its sides into the infamous urinal that Ernest salvaged from Sloppy Joe's Bar. The cats now use it as their watering hole.

A bridge crosses a pond, added since Hemingway's time, which leads past the swimming pool, Key West's first (Pauline paid twenty thousand dollars for it). Take a stroll under scarlet royal poinciana trees and date palms with fronds so long they almost touch the ground. At the end of the pool, under Ernest's studio, a yucca's trunk is so thick and sprawling it appears to be eons old.

It's fun to linger and to think about Pauline hiding eggs amidst the trees and flowers for her annual Easter egg hunt while peacocks strutted around. And Papa's friends came to the garden too, such as writer John Dos Passos, bullfighters, movie directors, and local fishing buddies, who sat around and shared tall tales. But most special of all is to think about the Pulitzer Prize–winning writer struggling over each word of the masterpieces he wrote in his studio overlooking the garden.

LOCATION: **907 Whitehead Street**

Casa Antigua, Hemingway's First Key West Residence

"Nothing is more the child of art than a garden."

—*Sir Walter Scott*

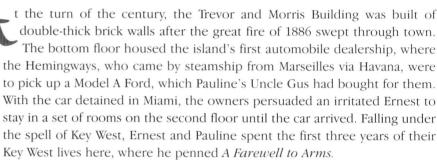

At the turn of the century, the Trevor and Morris Building was built of double-thick brick walls after the great fire of 1886 swept through town. The bottom floor housed the island's first automobile dealership, where the Hemingways, who came by steamship from Marseilles via Havana, were to pick up a Model A Ford, which Pauline's Uncle Gus had bought for them. With the car detained in Miami, the owners persuaded an irritated Ernest to stay in a set of rooms on the second floor until the car arrived. Falling under the spell of Key West, Ernest and Pauline spent the first three years of their Key West lives here, where he penned *A Farewell to Arms*.

The building went through a series of changes until a 1960 fire charred the interior. For years it sat in ruins. Just before the wrecking ball hit, Joe Worth bought it for twenty-six thousand dollars as a "great fixer upper" and inventively designed his family's three-story home around a huge atrium. His son, Tom Oosterhoudt, arrived in town to design one of the most unique gardens on the isle, jungly and exciting in its Indiana Jones attitude. The garden thrives in a hothouselike atmosphere behind the first floor shop, The Pelican Poop.

Tom, who later became city commissioner, felt from the start he wanted to plant in extreme ultratropicals for the look of a rainforest. So he lined the entrance in bromeliads, like the tri-colored neoregelia, and he filled the garden with his pride and joy, a collection of special heliconia, so symbolic of the tropics, with their huge leaves zooming past the second floor and adorned in bracts unequaled in shapes and color combinations

The "lagoon," the first black-bottomed pool in Key West, hosts a fountain imitating the lullaby of a steady rain. On one side, hot pink ti plants mark the hidden path to "Mayan ruins" where ancient-looking statues stand amidst fishtail ferns. Sand-dollar stepping stones lead to a Mayan fertility god reigning in a mystical corner. A carambola tree's star fruit drapes over the water; a dwarf royal poinciana is a knockout in its fiery colors.

With Hemingway's fascination for the jungle, perhaps he would have toasted the safari spirit of this garden, as well as the preservation of the building where he first fell in love with Key West.

LOCATION: **314 Simonton Street**

HERITAGE HOUSE MUSEUM AND ROBERT FROST COTTAGE

". . . go to the land of poetry."

—Johann Wolfgang von Goethe

There is a certain *je ne sais quoi* about the garden of the Heritage House Museum and Robert Frost Cottage. It is an original Key West garden, green, serene and spiritual as it sits atop an Indian shell midden behind the 1834 home built by seaman George Carey. The ancient, red brick hearth/ chimney of the separate cookhouse is now dressed up in pots of deep-red and yellow-green crotons, dieffenbachias, and antique owl andirons and is the centerpiece of this historical backyard.

The garden feels as though it's filled with the spirits of others who came to these grounds in earlier times, including Calusa Indians and dastardly pirates, who valued the fresh water from the underground stream. In the 1930s, fifth-generation Key Wester Jessie Porter, great-granddaughter of William Curry, bought the house and invited friends to the garden, many of whom are celebrated people of the twentieth century. She persuaded Robert Frost to winter in her garden cottage. Playwright Tennessee Williams came often. Philosopher John Dewey spent many afternoons here enjoying Jessie's

mix of people, including fan dancer Sally Rand, actress Tallulah Bankhead, and other poets, playwrights, and authors such as Thornton Wilder, Archibald MacLeish, Wallace Stevens, James Leo Herlihy, and, of course, the Hemingways.

When the city discarded the old bricks of its streets, Pauline and Jessie hauled truckloads back to their homes. Jessie created the patio and planting borders that wrap around ancient trees, including a Spanish lime tree, coconut palms, a tropical almond tree, and the gumbo limbo, which has been entwined with a seagrape tree forever. A double-decker treehouse used to be perched high in the gumbo limbo's boughs. Jessie's daughter, Jeane, who still lives on the premises, played there with local kids, including the Hemingway boys.

"That tree is still my best friend," Jeane says.

Great things hang from the trunks of these old trees—antiquities such as an iron candle chandelier and an ornate ladle holding a melted candle, probably left over from a recent poetry reading. The bare branches of a Confederate jasmine drip silvery Spanish moss, silver-green air plants, and orchids.

The almond tree is draped in Spanish moss too and is surrounded with bromeliads and vines of all kinds, deep-red crotons, and fishtail ferns. A large scallop shell sits at the foot of a concrete table, whose base is a trio of seahorses. Ornate, white wrought-iron furniture looks gracious in the area where the old cookhouse once stood, a beautiful setting for weddings.

The Robert Frost cottage is unassuming, fronted in a variegated schefflera sprouting from an old iron urn and a coral rock planter filled with mother-in-law tongues and corn plants. The four-time Pulitzer Prize winner spent many winters here overlooking and, no doubt, being inspired by this verdant scene. He would be proud to know that the annual Robert Frost Poetry Celebration, a day of readings by local poets, ends in a candlelit reception in the garden where he spent so many hours sharing thoughts with his friend, Miss Jessie.

LOCATION: **410 Caroline Street**

THE OLDEST HOUSE AND WRECKER'S MUSEUM

"First flower of their wilderness, star of their night."

—Samuel Gilman

The spirit of the island's first settlers pervades the Oldest House in Key West (circa 1829), which hosts the Wrecker's Museum and the Rosemary Austin Memorial Garden. The venerable free-standing cookhouse off the back porch is a historical treasure with its beehive oven, one of only two still existing today in the state of Florida. It sets the pioneering tone of the whole backyard.

It is fitting that so many beds of periwinkles embellish the garden, as they were among the first flowers planted by lady pioneers craving a bit of color around their little homes. They flower thick in white and purple, along with golden lantanas, at the foot of a young Bismarck palm and also around the lignum vitae, a native hardwood tree that may have greeted the island's first settlers. These seafarers are honored by a huge, rusty, antique anchor lying amidst bromeliads and the pretty cut-out leaves of monsteras.

Aging Spanish lime trees provide a shady canopy as well as candy-sweet fruit in perimeter plantings that also include papaya trees laden with fruit and an assortment of bananas, like the variegated red banana trees with wine-colored underleaves, fronted by thickets of purple porterweed, red hibiscus, walking iris, and dwarf royal poincianas. The Jamaican Tall coconut palm is what island dreams are made of, and many weddings and special events have been celebrated under its arching trunk crowned with twelve-foot-long fronds. It is heavy with coconuts: early settlers ate the coconut meat, quenched their thirst with coconut water, and turned the husks into mattress stuffing and rope. The vivid orange flowers of the Geiger tree, encircled in bright, curly-leafed crotons, are stunning behind the old cookhouse. Remnants of old freshwater wells swell with untamed wildflowers.

At the rear of the garden, history is revived in an exhibit dedicated to the wrecking profession, which made so many Key Westers wealthy. Ships' logs date back to 1841. Doll fragments are from a schooner that ran aground on the reef in 1880. Beautiful scrimshaw was carved in 1821, and a penny, minted between 1793 and 1857, was discovered on the grounds. It must be a lucky penny, for the old house, its cookhouse, and garden continue to bring pleasure to so many after long withstanding the forces of nature and time.

LOCATION: **322 Duval Street**

West Martello Tower and the Joe Allen Garden Center

"And new life blossoms in the ruins."

—*Johann Christoph Friedrich von Schiller*

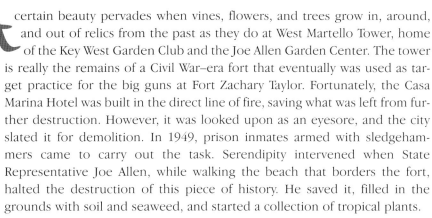

A certain beauty pervades when vines, flowers, and trees grow in, around, and out of relics from the past as they do at West Martello Tower, home of the Key West Garden Club and the Joe Allen Garden Center. The tower is really the remains of a Civil War–era fort that eventually was used as target practice for the big guns at Fort Zachary Taylor. Fortunately, the Casa Marina Hotel was built in the direct line of fire, saving what was left from further destruction. However, it was looked upon as an eyesore, and the city slated it for demolition. In 1949, prison inmates armed with sledgehammers came to carry out the task. Serendipity intervened when State Representative Joe Allen, while walking the beach that borders the fort, halted the destruction of this piece of history. He saved it, filled in the grounds with soil and seaweed, and started a collection of tropical plants.

At the entrance to the garden, an old brick wall is awash in croton colors. Across from it is my favorite, a spectacular breadfruit tree with handsome, deeply lobed, waxy leaves and balls of lime-green, alligator-skinned fruit. Captain Bligh can be credited with bringing these beautiful Tahitian trees to the West Indies in 1793.

From here, there are arches to duck through and a maze of pathways to wander, filled with wonderful finds: hat-sized, burnt-orange hibiscus, cacti blooming in furry, five-pointed stars, and the shaving brush tree, named for its wispy, delicate pink flowers. Purple water lilies float on a pond surrounded by a rainbow of wildflowers. A sea of bromeliads host a frangipani tree; Key lime trees are loaded with their famous, little, yellow limes; and an arbor is roofed in the golden, goblet-shaped flowers of the chalice vine, which releases the scent of coconut at night.

A sugary-white gazebo, trimmed in conch shell gingerbread, sits high on a hill overlooking the Atlantic Ocean. It's the perfect place to enjoy a picnic or brown bag lunch surrounded in sea lavender, beach sunflowers, orange firebush, beach daisies, and silver thatch palms. A succulent garden of cacti, century plants, and kalanchoe thrives unnerved by the sea and sun. And then there is a seaside "palm walk," with buccaneer, coconut, and seashore palms.

This hideaway from the rest of the world is so romantic, it is the setting for many weddings. For everyone, it is a place of beauty amidst the ruins of a fort built to help keep our nation united as one.

LOCATION: **White Street at the Atlantic Ocean**

Donkey Milk House

"As in a soul remembering good friends."

—*Shakespeare*

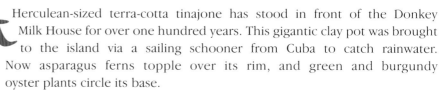

A Herculean-sized terra-cotta tinajone has stood in front of the Donkey Milk House for over one hundred years. This gigantic clay pot was brought to the island via a sailing schooner from Cuba to catch rainwater. Now asparagus ferns topple over its rim, and green and burgundy oyster plants circle its base.

The 1866 home was built by Peter Williams to accommodate his family of nine. Every day, cows' milk was dropped off, then picked up by a line of milkmen who filled up their donkey carts to head out and make their home deliveries. This history so fascinated Denison Tempel, who had been a Key West innkeeper, that he bought the house, restored it, and furnished it with his collection of period antiques. But the restoration depleted his funds before he was able to landscape the yard. So Denison's became a "garden of gifts," cuttings, seedlings, and pup plants donated by his friends. For months, he planted tiny bits of green on barren land, and friends teased him about his charming "bonsai garden." But not for long, for in this magical climate it took only two years for the "bonsais" to grow into a dense, tropical landscape.

Sun-bleached scallop shells, which beautifully reflect the moonlight, cover unplanted sitting areas. Encircling these areas is a lavish patchwork of greens, with smatterings of reds from chenille plants' fuzzy cattails, croton leaves, and ruffly hibiscus. The most unusual plant may be the suede plant, its lanky, knotted trunk topped with frilly-edged, velvety-suede leaves that are irresistible to touch. And, of course, antique red donkey cart wheels are prizes displayed throughout.

The collection of fruit trees serves as a delicious reminder of older island days. The custardy fruit of the sugar apple was turned into ice cream and milk shakes, and delectable syrups were made from soursops. The tall, thin papaya trees are topped with clusters of leaves and tropical fruit. A carambola is decorated with its five-ribbed fruit, a Barbados cherry flashes red polka dots, and the Madagascar almond is laden with nuts.

When the Donkey Milk House was open to the public for touring, it impressed thousands of visitors from all over the world. Unfortunately, the tours have been suspended, but it is not out of the question that the house and garden may be reopened one day. In the meantime, Denison continues the spirit in which his garden was sown by passing on his seedlings, cuttings, and pups to others who are looking to grow a garden whose life comes from the gifts of friends.

LOCATION: **613 Eaton Street**

Awaken unto the Gardens

THE MARQUESA HOTEL

"Paradise is where I am."

—*Voltaire*

The award-winning courtyard garden of the small, luxury Marquesa Hotel is reason in itself to come to Key West. It is a marriage of exquisite plantings, a romantic, tiered waterfall, and the serenity of quiet seclusion. The signature aqua main building was built in 1864 as a private residence and later turned into a boardinghouse, where it is rumored Gloria Swanson spent some of her childhood years. If so, her playground was the garden of today.

The original pool area presents a wall of wine- and cream-colored allamandas and a trio of travelers-trees with white, birdlike blooms. Their bases are enshrouded in Burle Marx philodendron, cardboard palms, and leather ferns. The trunks of Carpentaria palms are loaded with orchids, which also grace each guest room. This is just the prelude to the "second" garden, designed by landscape architect Raymond Jungles, which the Florida Chapter of the American Society of Landscape Architects honored with an Award of Excellence.

The entrance to the second garden is marked by a swirling-leafed screw pine tree that grows in a circular bed. Its sculptural trunk is steeped in bromeliads blooming in long coral-pinks. More orchids hang from its branches in wooden baskets while others cling to limbs. To luxuriate in a massage in the shade of this island setting is pure indulgence.

I love strolling the garden that surrounds the swimming pool and sneaks into every little corner of the cottages, newly constructed in Old Key West architectural style. A bold specimen of a Fiji fan palm, with its large pleated fronds, is ultra-islandy, as are the green bamboolike trunks of Cabada palms and a magnificent triangle palm bathed in a base of sherbet-orange ixoras. Off in a little corner of its own, a lattice wall is covered with pots and pots of orchids and bromeliads sporting sumptuous blooms of all colors. In another secret niche, a thick gathering of heliconia is a sight to behold, with its half-hidden orange and yellow-orange blooms, and pots of bromeliads are perched on the end of each step of a stairway, creating a rising wall of tropicals.

An old man palm sits in a bed of wildly growing coral creeper across from deep-red "Calypso Queen" Hawaiian cordylines. Creeping ficus steals across the stairs as well as the walls, which encircle an elevated waterfall garden. It is a climb edged in Spanish shawl to where water spills over three tiers, echoing a rain shower. Toddy fishtail palms grow over four stories high, their "feet" enveloped in bromeliads and pink ginger.

"We take our garden very seriously," says Carol Wightman, owner and general manager of this AAA four-diamond hotel. From what I saw, that may be an understatement.

LOCATION: **600 Fleming Street**

HERON HOUSE

"I can always tell when someone is coming down with orchid fever. The first symptom is pure amazement."

—*Anonymous*

Beyond the long, lanky branches of fuchsia bougainvillea toppling over the walls of the Heron House lies a treasure of over one thousand orchids. They cling to the trunks of Christmas palms, scheffleras, and queen palms; peek out through thick monstera that climbs a gumbo limbo tree; and hang from fishtail palms in wooden baskets. Many adorn guest rooms. Most are beautifully displayed in an orchid cottage brimming with unusual species as well as favorite hybrids.

This collection, representative of both Old World and New World tropics, is cherished and nurtured by co-owner Robert Framarin. His passion for orchids started in 1982 en route to a Key West vacation. A chance stop at Homestead's Orchid Jungle, where he purchased his first, a miniature orange cattleya, changed his life. Since that encounter, orchids are tied into every journey, whether to buy plants at a California nursery or to admire them in the wild in Hawaii or Thailand. Since he is adamant about preserving orchids in their native habitat, his is a first-class collection born from seedlings he has bought and nurtured for close to twenty years. It gives Robert great joy to share their beauty.

Originally the orchids were housed in a screened-in box. Because everyone kept following Robert around to get a peek at the blooms, he decided to create a customized, cedar-slatted cottage designed to meet all of the needs of his orchids, which have become the signature of this AAA four-diamond boutique hotel. When the cottage door is open, guests are welcome to savor this enviable private collection, which represents a tour de force of nature's most exotic colors and shapes, changing, of course, with what is blooming at the moment.

Among the most stunning is a cymbidium, its chartreuse flowers flaunting a white lip tinged in pink as they dangle from a three-foot flower spike. One of the easiest to identify is the lady slipper. Rare and stunning is the pink flush of the white bloom of Eulophellia Rolsei, a hybrid of two species, which grows in the screw pine forests of the Seychelles. And then there is the largest, Southeast Asia's Tiger orchid, boasting fifty spectacular, four-inch, yellow blooms mottled in deep reddish-brown.

The collection is displayed with gardening antiques. An orchid grows within each square of old-fashioned milk bottle carriers, the kind milkmen used to carry to Grandma's house. The charm of simpler times is also reflected in Robert's collection of antiquated watering cans and a pair of old black clippers, which hang in a place of honor, a valued heirloom his grandfather brought from Italy long ago. Now they shine amidst his grandson's world class orchid collection thriving in Key West.

For Robert, this garden is a labor of love.

LOCATION: **512 Simonton Street**

THE MERMAID &
THE ALLIGATOR

". . . and little birds which sing very sweetly."

—Christopher Columbus

There is something special about a garden where birds sing, whether finches and lovebirds scattered about in pretty cages or palm warblers who fly in to feed on Chinese fan palm berries. Their aria blends with soft classical music, falling water, and the wind brushing the aged trees—date palms, sapodillas, and a high-headed mahogany.

Guests relax on the front verandah of the house built in 1904 by Mr. Malone, city attorney. It overlooks an enviable front yard, a gift from the 1909 hurricane, which blew the house back from its streetside foundation.

Out back the lower garden is "Key West charming" with a fanciful chandelier dangling from a royal poinciana tree. It twirls in the breeze, its prisms catching the sun, adding diamonds of dancing light to palms and heliconias. Orchids hang from orange jasmine trees, and trickles of water float down a deep-blue tiled wall into a fish pond.

A few steps up, a statue of a mermaid tenderly kissing an alligator overlooks a sapphire plunge pool framed in whispy palms. A Hawaiian spirit prevails with pineapple plants, special banana trees (from dwarf to forty-foot-tall black fruit varieties), and a rare yellow poinciana tree.

I tarried at each venue, savoring the sounds, spying on butterflies and birds, and relishing the sunlight as it waltzed through the gardens reminiscent of the tropical aura of Maui.

LOCATION: **729 Truman Avenue**

ISLAND CITY HOUSE HOTEL

"Amidst the tall ancestral trees . . ."

—Felicia Dorothea Hemans

In 1889, a wealthy Charleston merchant built a two-story Victorian beauty and moved in with his family. When news came of a railroad that would link the southernmost city with the rest of the world, he added a third story and opened the island's first hotel. Today, as the Island City House Hotel, it is the oldest operating hotel in Key West. A sunny "gardenette" out front, alive with purple porterweed and red firecracker plants, signals the scene within: an L-shaped garden—cool and comfy in its old-time Keys feel—which links the three tiers of verandahs and ornate gingerbread of the main building to the merchant's carriage house, the only one of its kind remaining on the island.

One can just imagine the wealthy Charlestonian at the reins of his horses, bringing home the family under the crescent moon of the carriage house's wooden arch. They probably walked past some of these same old trees, maybe stopping to pluck an avocado, Key lime, or fruit of the sapodilla while strolling to the house. The children possibly played where I sat contentedly under a frangipani tree on black, wrought-iron chairs in the breakfast area. A coral-rock fountain rained into a little pond, where goldfish shimmered as the sun happened upon them. I thought of John F. Kennedy, who, as a young Navy man, stayed here and roamed these same grounds.

But this is also a garden where you should look "up" to the trees so tall their leaves always whisper in even the slightest of breezes. The canopy is green and woodsy with branches of venerable Spanish limes, sapodilla, buttonwood, and autograph trees, plus an assortment of palms. A golden shower tree bathes the hideaway in cascades of deep-yellow flowers and in the aroma of chocolate from its cocoa-colored seed pods.

Below is a mountain of hundreds of bromeliads flashing red, purple, pink, burgundy, and yellow beside a nocturnally blooming cereus cactus. It looms over red and orange heliconia and white birds of paradise accented by an old-fashioned Charleston-style street lamp.

It's a special, old Key West garden, whose rarest plant is the insect-catching pelican flower, its immature blooms resembling brown pelicans. It is also a garden where children stroll, as this is one of only a handful of Old Town guest houses where children are welcome and can find their own special places within the garden's secret corners.

LOCATION: **411 William Street**

4FT

THE PARADISE INN

"A garden is a lovesome thing . . . ."
—Thomas Edward Brown

Brazilian, Cherries Jubilee allamandas shape the entry to the Paradise Inn. Lanky branches of the ylang-ylang tree bow to my approach, bejeweled in pale-yellow flowers. They are just the first showstoppers in this award-winning garden, designed by landscape architect Raymond Jungles.

Bright pink bougainvillea blankets an old gumbo limbo tree all the way to its top. Beyond, guest rooms are embellished in the South Seas look of the large, pleated leaves of Fiji fan palms, pink hibiscus, and a wall ablaze with the Tahitian shrub, "Match me if you can." Within these plantings are local artist John Martini's metal sculptures, which add a capriciousness to the garden.

When I reached the tropical courtyard, the air was filled with the hypnotic sound of a heavy rain. Its source: water steadily flowing from the beaks of bronze cranes that landed poolside. Its backdrop is a wall of towering, grand-leafed relatives: travelers-trees, white birds of paradise, bananas, and heliconia. Across the pool is a mass of magnificent red ginger that looks like a postcard from its homeland, the South Pacific. It melds into a bed of Confederate jasmine, African king's mantle, lavender-pink bougainvillea, and solitaire palms growing past second-floor balconies.

Between the pool's deep end and the Jacuzzi is an island of coral rock that frames a lily pond flowering in passion purple. Unusually large bromeliads from Brazil grow as neighbors to amazing, purple-leaf crinum lilies, whose giant rosettes of pointed leaves loom six feet tall. Beneath, yellow kalanchoe covers the ground. Scattered about are great specimens of trees, from red latan palms native to Mauritius to African sausage trees, with their night-blooming, wine-colored flowers.

This many-faceted garden goes on and on, embracing every inch of the grounds in tropical splendor, color, and tranquil beauty. It is a place to feast your eyes on rarely seen tropicals, each labeled for easy identification, like a grand museum filled with tropical art.

LOCATION: **819 Simonton Street**

THE GARDENS HOTEL

"Our passion is our task."

—Henry James

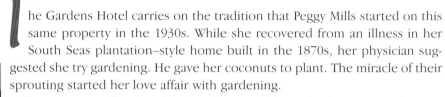

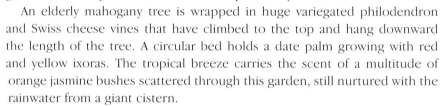

The Gardens Hotel carries on the tradition that Peggy Mills started on this same property in the 1930s. While she recovered from an illness in her South Seas plantation–style home built in the 1870s, her physician suggested she try gardening. He gave her coconuts to plant. The miracle of their sprouting started her love affair with gardening.

Peggy began collecting clippings from neighbors. As she ran out of space, she annexed adjacent properties, leveling thirteen structures and perfecting a garden boasting a world-class collection of orchids and rare bamboo. She passed on in the '70s, but the soul of her hobby is alive in this intimate hotel, where, just off the back porch, grows a wild, jungly introduction to the grounds, whose path of red bricks once paved city streets.

An elderly mahogany tree is wrapped in huge variegated philodendron and Swiss cheese vines that have climbed to the top and hang downward the length of the tree. A circular bed holds a date palm growing with red and yellow ixoras. The tropical breeze carries the scent of a multitude of orange jasmine bushes scattered through this garden, still nurtured with the rainwater from a giant cistern.

A little pond, a remnant of another cistern, was used by Ernest and Pauline Hemingway to cool off when visiting Peggy on hot days. It is said to have inspired Pauline to install Key West's first swimming pool at the Hemingway home.

The showpieces of Peggy's legacy are mammoth, Cuban tinajones over one hundred years old. In the 1800s, it took Cuban potters seven years to make a single piece. Peggy used her influence to arrange to have the huge clay pots shipped here in the 1950s, when Batista was in power. They were hauled by oxcart from Hamaguey to Havana, then barged to Miami and filled with dirt, which she spread in her garden once they arrived. Originally used as cisterns, they lie on their sides beneath bamboo palms so they won't fill up with water.

Wild birds, especially doves, fly through a sky-high canopy of venerable trees, including Spanish limes, sour oranges, tamarinds, African tulips, and a rare balsa wood tree, exotic with its big, leathery leaves. The fishtail palms are thought to be the oldest on the isle.

People still do all kinds of things to steal a view of the garden behind the high fence, just as they did in the days of Peggy Mills, but guests have the special privilege of sipping cool cocktails at the pool bar, surrounded by the beauty of Peggy's garden.

LOCATION: **526 Angela Street**

THE PIER HOUSE RESORT AND CARIBBEAN SPA

" I like to walk about amidst the beautiful things. . . ."

—George Santayana

The expansive garden of the Pier House is Caribbean magic, but it wasn't designed that way. It just evolved over the years from the imagination of everyone who has worked here, including art students from New York whose creativity was unleashed while working with tropical plants.

Bold Chinese bamboo towers at the entrance before a fantasia of bromeliads, running and clumping in a mass along the ground, others draping the trunk of an old Norfolk pine. They send forth spectacular flower spikes ranging from pale-pinks with spots of purple-blue to reds, yellows, and even apricots. In a special little corner an old gumbo limbo tree's portly branches sport a handsome staghorn fern and lots of blooming orchids. More bromeliads hover over a miniature water garden whose stream trickles around yellow canna lilies, dramatic elephant ears, and an elkhorn fern.

Patches of Xanadu philodendrons lead to a bed of anthuriums, including long ruffly leaves of bird's nests. The anthuriums grow in the shade of palms, along with a prized red fern, discovered at Big Pine Key's flea market.

Magnificent specimens of bottle palms, the garden's two mascots, grow near the beach bar. They are stunning, with their stout, gray trunks bulging near their bases in perfect bottle shapes. Throughout is a jewel box of pretty plants: gingers; white birds of paradise; firecracker plants weeping a mass of red; an aged, long-armed cereus cactus; thick heliconia; and towering, beachside coconut palms, under which couples await sunset to say "I do."

So wander the walkways in a relaxed spirit, peeking into the nooks and crannies where hidden gardens grow.

LOCATION: **One Duval Street**

THE DUVAL HOUSE

". . . as green as emerald."

—Samuel Taylor Coleridge

An emerald oasis awaits behind the Duval House, cooled by the dense canopy of one-hundred-year-old banyan trees, Spanish limes, and coconut palms. In rain-forest fashion, pothos vines have climbed the trees' trunks into the canopy. Beneath is a sea of ferns (fishtails, leather leafs, and Bostons) that waver in just a breath of air. These ancient plants, which have flourished on our planet for over three hundred million years, add a graceful, Victorian look to the grounds, lying low and arching over the maroon brick walkway.

Hibiscus, the epitome of tropical flowers, is revered here as in Malaysia, where it is the national flower, and in Hawaii, where it is the state flower. Within the garden are more than thirty varieties in a palette of colors, from creamy white with dark-red centers to delicate pinks and fire-engine reds. Some are large single blossoms, others more ruffly as double or triple bloomers within a single flower. Guests are welcomed by hibiscus flowers placed on their pillows, freshly picked right outside their doors.

This verdant garden, also rich in yuccas, Christmas palms, crinum lilies, and heliconia, is encircled in the quiet romance of snow-white, gingerbread-bedecked houses rooted in the cigar era of the late 1800s. The twin houses were boardinghouses where cigar workers' families lived, and the A-frame was a warehouse where Cuban tobacco was stored. This nostalgic ambiance is carried over to the diamond of the garden, a pretty Victorian gazebo, its tin roof sparkly and its interior comfy with a wicker couch, perfect for napping or snuggling up with a good book. Steps away is a hammock for two, in which lovers succumb to its gentle sway. Pennies and dimes, tossed in as people make wishes, glitter in the bottom of a fishless pond. Two verdigris cranes peer out over the garden, souvenirs of the owner's trips to Thailand, as are the Asian-style birdcages along the garden walk.

It is hard to imagine that this idyllic spot is right off Duval Street. Back here in the garden, the busy street seems worlds away.

LOCATION: **815 Duval Street**

EATON LODGE

"The summer dream beneath the tamarind tree."

—*Edgar Allen Poe*

One of the first ornamental gardens on the Keys once grew around the Eaton Lodge. Genevieve Warren cultivated it at her charming 1886 Victorian mansion, where she and her physician husband, William, raised their family, along with her impressive orchid collection.

Genevieve laid old red brick as pathways and borders around circular planting areas, and she had topsoil barged in from Florida's Panhandle. She planted all kinds of trees, from which she hung orchids and whose bases she crowded with bromeliads. She transformed an old cistern into a fish pond encircled with plants. The Warrens then built an unheard-of three-story cistern—which remains at the rear of the inn today—to ensure water for her garden, his practice, and their lifestyle.

After the property left the Warren family, one of its owners ripped out Genevieve's precious plantings save for a few trees, planted an unsuccessful formal English garden, then bricked over the entire yard. Eventually, the home was abandoned and vandalized, and the remaining of Genevieve's prized orchids were chopped out of trees and sold cheaply on the street. Along came Carolyn and Stephen West, who were seemingly lured to Key West to keep Genevieve's spirit alive. They restored the home as a bed-and-breakfast and scoured the garden with sticks, poking through the bricks in search of the soil of Genevieve's original flower beds. The bricks were removed and the beds replanted.

It's a good feeling to walk in Genevieve's footsteps through the garden she once tended. Some of the trunks of the ancient trees still maintain "halos" from where her orchids tenaciously gripped. Her Brazilian jacaranda tree is ultra-feminine, with its lacy leaflets and springtime blooms of soothing blue bell–shaped flowers. When they float down on the currents of the wind, they magically create a bluish-purple carpet on the ground below. The Wests have painted the shutters and doors of the lodge a perfectly matched jacaranda color.

The two massive tamarind trees, native to India, may be the best specimens on the isle, and they bear rust-brown pods encasing pulp, which locals turn into candy, preserves, and ice cream. Genevieve's Key lime trees have grown three stories tall. Her immense Spanish lime now grows through the roof of a small room added on to the house at some point.

Oh, and Genevieve's fish pond? Water spills down the tiers of a pretty little fountain into the pond framed in bromeliads and conch shells. Its trickle can be heard out on the street, beyond the mass of purple-pink bougainvillea that blankets the black, antique, wrought-iron fence. Genevieve would approve, I'm sure.

LOCATION: **511 Eaton Street**

SIMONTON COURT HISTORIC INN AND COTTAGES

"The memory be green."

—*Shakespeare*

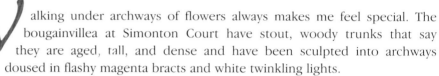

Walking under archways of flowers always makes me feel special. The bougainvillea at Simonton Court have stout, woody trunks that say they are aged, tall, and dense and have been sculpted into archways doused in flashy magenta bracts and white twinkling lights.

Wandering this garden, which all are welcome to do, is like discovering a little village that offers tastes of different social statuses of earlier eras with gardens to match. The inn is an 1870 cigar factory, where tobacco leaves were stored and dried on the second floor and rolled and sold on the first. Its side is graced with colorful crotons, the purplish-pink flowers of an orchid tree, and, of course, the arching bougainvillea. Behind, surrounding a black-bottom pool framed in black lobster traps used as tables for oil lamps, are hot-pink oleanders and its botanical cousin, yellow allamandas.

Across the walkway is a nook with the look of the French Quarter, with a private *jardin* of red and yellow ixoras, blue daze, yellow allamandas, and a cluster of Chinese fan palms. Down the lane, a tall coconut palm and frilly Ming araleas mark the cottage "neighborhood." Once the homes of cigar rollers, the pink-and-white houses are accented with plantings of banana trees, ficus hedges, grand clumps of bamboo, pink ginger, and blue sky vines.

Flashy bougainvillea frames the view of the white mansion, two stories of gingerbread grandeur built by a judge who entertained in high style in his second-floor ballroom. It overlooks the aqua pool, whose old brick corners are all that remain of the cistern that once caught water in this very spot. A trio of travelers-trees grows on one side of the pool, and an impressive Savannah palm towers sixty feet tall on the other. Beyond is a grove of banana trees, the gorgeous red and orange-yellow blooms of Flame heliconia, and, of course, lush bougainvillea.

A gardenia bush blesses the poolside breakfast area with its sweet scent. In an inconspicuous corner stands a noble Bismarck palm, with its starburst, silvery blue-green leaves. Owner Mrs. Moloney chose the tree as a loving, living memorial to her late husband because of its appearance—strong, bright stars with spark and spirit—just like Richard D. Moloney, whose vision created Simonton Court so many years ago.

LOCATION: **320 Simonton Street**

Tiny Gardens and a Grand Collection

An Artist's Palette of Flowers

"More than anything, I must have flowers,
always, always."

—*Claude Monet*

Everyone dreams of a house behind a white picket fence, where flowers in more colors than an artist's palette drape over and peep through the evenly spaced slats. Artist Richard Matson has such a garden.

"It's a work always in progress," Richard told me one morning as he swept the brick patio with a homemade broom of dried Christmas palm fronds banded together with masking tape. "These particular fronds have an electric affinity for the things I'm sweeping up, especially those little seed pods that drop from the Washingtonians. If I used a regular broom, I'd be here all day."

The two Washingtonian palms were planted within cutouts in the brick, which he collected on bike runs around the isle, then laid himself. Spindle palms frame the steps to his home, which was built in 1890. His flower garden encircles it all. One would never know this lush collage of flowers beneath coconut palms is a container garden whose secret is to camouflage every smidgen of dirt and container in color.

Within the garden grow golden dewdrops, seasonally drenched in either small lavender flowers or golden, pearl-like berries; deeper purple porter-weed; and red, spicy jatropha with their lively, yellow centers. The princess plant blooms purple near a bird of paradise Richard rescued from a Key West

trash heap. Red ixoras mingle with brighter red hibiscus and snow-white pinwheel jasmine, its waxy, lime-colored leaves contrasting with rich, red canna lilies. A gorgeous white hibiscus with bing cherry–red centers blooms alongside pink mandevilles and coral gingers, while a dwarf royal poinciana, neon-bright in red-orange and yellow, mixes with the perky, fronded, European fan palms, junglelike heliconia, and the delicacy of a pale, peach-pink Jamaican dogwood.

Each evening, about two hours before sunset, Richard fills the basket of his bike with paints, brushes, and easel and rides off to paint the gingerbread-trimmed houses of Old Town in the vivid colors unique to his style, immortalizing many of these grand old homes—and their gardens of the moment.

LOCATION: **1311 Olivia Street**

A CARIBBEAN FLING

"... to imagine is everything."

—Anatole France

The soul of Barry Archung and Jan Schoenmaker's garden is so Caribbean I could almost hear the steel drums playing. It is a tiny place, bursting with lively color and character, and it is evidence that when it comes to great gardens, size just doesn't matter.

Vanda, dendrobium, and phaleanopsis orchids, and a variety of bromeliads hang on woven bamboo stretched as a privacy wall the length of the dining room/breezeway. Its colorful table is decked out in blooming orchids and large wooden bowls of fresh tropical fruit. A little, potted old man palm marks the spot where I could either climb a ladder to a rooftop sundeck or step into the pint-sized garden, where an elderly avocado tree stands with orchids galore growing from its branches and bark. Beside the tree is a reproduction of a fifteenth-century Italian Della Robia tile, which adds a touch of European elegance.

A tiny palm garden runs the distance between the avocado tree and the kitchen, which is separate from the house, as in olden days. The garden overflows with little trees that add color and vitality—red bananas with their underleaves flashing rich burgundy in the breeze, a metallic palm with an

intense sheen, the scarlet trunk of a lipstick palm, the blue-green of a buccaneer, the glitter of dwarf silver saw palmetto, the licuala's lime green leaves, the darker green needle palm, and the grayish trunk of a bottle palm.

A rare variegated monstera adds its uniqueness, as do the ruffles of a staghorn fern and the shininess of Burle Marx philodendron. Oyster shells shimmer as ground cover. A fallen, tree trunk reaches over the sapphire plunge pool, which is blanketed in bromeliads, more orchids, and Spanish moss. The tiny jungle seems to go on forever into the neighboring yard. But it's only an illusion created by a mirror ingeniously held fast in tracks installed along the fence. Barry and Jan borrowed the idea from Pennsylvania's celebrated Longwood Gardens.

A lively mural painted in bright greens and yellows brings tropical vines to the back outer wall, which overlooks the pool of the 1888 shipwright's house. Everything else is painted in the Caribbean colors of bright, bold raspberry, cadmium yellow, and green-black. It's quite a place to hang out—island-style. Just bring on the reggae, rum punch, and conch fritters!

LOCATION: **707 Southard Street**

A Garden of Gratitude

". . . beauty without extravagance."

—*Thucydides*

There is a greatness within the pocket-sized backyard of Michael Reece that reflects the heart that went into its planting. Because he rents a little house that sits on a quiet lane, his is a container garden filled with favorite plants and personal treasures that can travel with him through life.

When Michael moved in, he avoided the dark backyard overgrown with messy trees. As years passed, he cut them back, which gave sunlight to a venerable, night-blooming cereus cactus, the only plant in the garden that grows from the ground. Thought to be over thirty years old, this "Queen of the Night" stands twenty feet tall, its fleshy, ribbed arms branching wildly skyward. To behold its nocturnal blooming of ivory flowers centered in golden yellow is a privilege, as more than one hundred flowers fill the midnight breeze with the scent of vanilla. But they're fleeting, withering in the first light of dawn. Beneath the "lady" is a copper metal sculpture of a bird of paradise that means the world to Michael since the friend who created it has since passed on. Twenty-one years after his friend made the sculpture, Michael walked into the yard of the owner, who miraculously gave it to Michael as a gift.

"It's amazing how fate takes you places," Michael says. "It's such a blessing to have this in my garden."

Surrounding the sculpture are decorative pots of all sizes and at all levels, filled with plants of the tropics such as big-leafed bananas, coconuts, and fan palms. But my eye was enticed by the bright-red stripe within the pleated leaves of an immature red latan palm bought as a wee specimen for ten dollars at the Secret Garden's palm sale six years ago. Encircling the palms is a picture of textures, shapes, and colors: black cardinal plants, Boston and asparagus ferns, Xanadus, miniature red powderpuffs, and ginger. A spicy jatropha rests high on a gorgeous birdbath Michael rescued from a Key West trash heap. Banded tulip and helmet shells have special places, and rocks scattered among the pots are ones he has collected on travels to national parks all across America. There's even some lava that Michael picked up in Hawaii.

An orchid more than ten years old hangs on the fence beside an enviable wind chime that Michael made from antique glass bottle tops etched by the sand and sea like beach glass. He collected the colorful glass years ago on a special Key West beach. It now hangs suspended from driftwood and blesses him with a subtle, unique song.

As we sat in his garden, listening to the soft tingle of the chimes and the jungly *wukwow* of geckos, Michael reminisced about hitchhiking from Houston to Key West over twenty-four years ago with absolutely nothing.

"I feel very lucky to have what I have," he said, looking around his tiny backyard.

LOCATION: **1122 Stump Lane**

OF FLOWERS AND VINES

"Small cheer and great welcome makes a merry feast."

—Shakespeare

Michael Pelkey has a radiant, miniature garden in sunny yellow and white. It sits behind his 520-square foot home, which has been applauded as "The Littlemost House" in Key West and featured on Home & Garden Television more than once. It is easy to spot, with its five black crow silhouettes roosting on the gleaming tin roof. When Michael financed the purchase of his then shell-of-a-structure on his credit card, friends were shocked. It was a place only a man who thinks in terms of "not what is but what could be" would love. Now his home and garden turn heads.

Michael escorted me to his garden through his classy-cute house, past his collection of two hundred pudding molds and a velvet, high-backed couch and through his French country kitchen. French doors open onto a diminutive deck, where he entertains in high style amidst tropical vines. A rectangular table, whose cozy, L-shaped seating bench runs the length of his garden along the white picket fence, was exquisitely set for dinner for twelve. Blue sky vines and the unique, mottled, deep-burgundy flowers of unusual calico vines fill the open spaces between the fence and outer frame of the pergola over the table.

This is where Michael extends his little garden's charm with this famous "tablescapes." They change with every occasion, according to what is freshly blooming. The day I visited he was plucking white and blue passion flowers to adorn napkins elegantly placed on fine white china. A little votive candleholder held a red hibiscus at each setting. And Michael added yellow and green croton leaves to a large crystal vase of fresh flowers from the florist.

Steps away, bright yellow loveseats face each other, their end tables crowned with vases of fresh sunflowers. A stucco wall projects a swag of pinecones and acorns, symbolic of Michael's Bostonian roots. Fresh pineapples, the fruit of tropical hospitality, top the wall and are striking against a background of deep-green banana leaves. Below, an antique, bronze Chinese swan is a fountain from which water flows into a carved cement trough, painted black and framed in grapevine topiaries of creeping ficus.

The wall reaches across the garden to the tiny yet sophisticated guest house (once a tool shed), whose outside wall is etched with more creeping ficus stealing its way toward a Romanesque plaque of a lion's head. Red hibiscus and a stand of bananas conceal the guest house's outdoor shower.

This maybe the tiniest of gardens, but it is kingly in the magical moments remembered by all who have visited.

Michael also creates Key West Christmas magic in his front yard. Each year

he gathers red pepper berry branches and weaves them into garland accented with key limes, sour oranges, variegated red croton leaves, white starfish, sea urchins, and conch shells. The garland graces his white picket fence, whose posts are topped with fresh pineapples, which exude a tropical essence. His bicycle, "an old Conch cruiser," leans against the fence, its wicker basket holding a conical rosemary tree donned in tropical fruit, nuts, and starfish. It's a stunning Key West holiday tradition.

LOCATION: **532 Grinnell Street**

SOUTHERN COMFORT

"O, for a beaker full of the warm South . . ."

—Keats

The magnolia-white fence of the narrow street garden of Storm Haven, an 1865 Southern Colonial home, has a holy history. It is made from balustrades rescued from the old convent at St. Mary Star of the Sea. Its history accentuates both the little, formal garden as well as the house, which served as a shelter for neighbors during hurricanes.

Antique bricks still bearing the imprint "Baltimore" pave the garden area. They once served as ballast in schooners departing from that Northern port bound for the Keys. Beneath the columned porch of the eyebrow house are beds bright with blue plumbago, the real energy of the garden, tipped at each end with *Dracaena marginata* growing tall and capricious in free form. On the left side, a unique planting alternates hot-pink ti plants with bamboo palms.

The front edge of the garden is symmetrically planted, with each side of the gate mirroring the other in full rosettes of forest green sagos, their leaves extending between the balustrades. Airy fronds of pygmy date palms weep over the rail, more ti plants add their height and color, and curly-leafed crotons flash reds, greens, and yellows. Two royal palms exude tropical formality, and scallop shells covering the bare earth around the plants bring a flavor from the surrounding sea to a little garden reminiscent of the Deep South in summertime.

LOCATION: **525 Frances Street**

A SWEET STREET GARDEN

"The tree of life also in the midst of the garden."

—*Old Testament*

In 1870 Bahama-born wrecker, sponger, and city commissioner Benjamin Baker built the "Gingerbread House" as a wedding gift for his daughter. The house stayed in the family until 1972, the year a tornado came whipping through, blowing the house a few feet off its foundation, miraculously without any major damage to its structure.

Dreamsicle-colored and bathed in lacy gingerbread, elaborate friezes, and under-the-eaves brackets, it's veritable Key West. Today Robert and Tina Newman call it home. Their little street garden is a stunning example of the beauty and style of indigenous plants and trees. A showcase of lavender and rare Keys trees, the garden is lush in the soul of the old Florida Keys—the perfect compliment to the most decorated house on the island.

The long, flowing branches of the lignum vitae tree that tumble over the white picket fence are seasonally blanketed in either the little lavender blooms that Jamaica took as its national flower or in orange-yellow pods that burst open in bright red seeds. The seed pods are so abundant here that the Key West Botanical Garden Club collects them to propagate the slow-growing trees in hopes of securing their future. Many, however, fall to the ground, sprouting seedlings which Robert digs up and gives to visiting friends, who grow them as bonsais or in hothouse gardens from New Orleans to Austria.

The dense, heavy wood of lignum vitae is the only wood sold by the pound. It was fashioned into hinges on the Erie Canal, still functioning after one hundred years. Ancient writings imply that it was shaped into the Holy Grail, and it has been described as the mystical tree in the Garden of Eden. Overharvesting, which includes the US Navy's use of the tree's durable, unsinkable wood in submarine construction, has unfortunately rendered the lignum vitae an endangered species in the Florida Keys.

More lavender brightens the garden in both the unusual vortex plant, whose tiny pale flowers form the shape of King Neptune's fork, and in the deeper hues of porterweed. The silvery glint of the fanned leaves of silver palms contrast beautifully with the deep green Key thatch palms. A rare cluster of four buccaneer palms, with ringed, pale blue-green trunks, is gorgeous, as is the bottle palm with its perky fronds and swollen trunk. Below, the ground is covered with bromeliads, from small fireballs to the larger, broader-leafed *Vresia imperialis*.

"We hope others realize the special beauty you can create with an indigenous garden," Tina said. "And it's a lot less work than tending to exotics."

LOCATION: **615 Elizabeth Street**

Rare Palms of Cuba

"... rarer gifts than gold."

—Rupert Brooke

Peter Whelan is famous in the music world for his efforts to preserve the jazz and blues of the 1920s and '30s and for his work as editor and publisher of *78 Quarterly*, a magazine devoted to keeping this old-time music alive. In the world of palms, he is known for his botanically significant collection of rare palms, which includes the palms of Cuba, the *Copernicia* genus. So his home is enveloped in a garden of palms, a fantasia of strange and exciting trees so fabulous in their beauty and sizes they took my breath away.

Peter finds many of his specimens at Miami's Fairchild Tropical Garden, especially at their palm collectors sale, where determined palm lovers have managed to get *Copernicia* seeds from German collectors who travel to Cuba.

"*Copernicia* are among the slowest growing of all palms," Peter says. "That's why you never see them in nurseries. Hardly anyone wants to wait for them to grow." But those who do wait are rewarded with some of nature's most spectacular artistry. My introduction began with *Copernicia macroglossa*, also known as the Cuban petticoat palm, which palm aficionados consider one of the most spectacular of all. Its fanlike leaves are loosely packed, seemingly without stems, and spiral in great, concentric circles. As these unique leaves fade, they turn golden tan and droop downward right on top of one another, creating layers of petticoats extending to the ground. *Copernicia rigida*, a product of the Cuban coastline, looks as novel as its cousin but with leaves that are more rigid and upright. They are true tropical enchantment.

The *Copernicia baileyana* has a gigantic trunk, leaf bases, and fan-shaped fronds as big as sails. Its thirty- to forty-foot stems are stout and edged in black, razor-sharp teeth. When the wind blows through its leaves, it sounds as if sailboats are tacking into the wind. Then there is *Copernicia hospita*, with its mysterious silver seeds, the *cowellii*, which is small yet pretty with its waxy, white underleaves, and the *fallaense*, which is majestic with the largest leaves of all, plus an impressive array of hybrids.

Peter's "alley" is a nursery of seedlings, babies that he prizes and nurtures. Like any member of the International Palm Society, he can't resist other masterpieces of nature, so his palm garden also includes a collection of uncommon licuala; a fabulous bamboo called *Bamboosa vulgaris;* the world's largest anthurium; a great fern growing from a hot tub–sized pot; and palms sporting thorns so wicked they could be deadly weapons.

I felt honored to have walked among so many extraordinary palms, which so few people ever have a chance to see.

LOCATION: **626 Canfield Lane**

The Gardens of Old Town

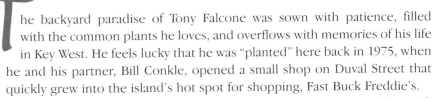

A Garden of Key West Memories

"A man's homeland is wherever he prospers."

—*Aristophanes*

The backyard paradise of Tony Falcone was sown with patience, filled with the common plants he loves, and overflows with memories of his life in Key West. He feels lucky that he was "planted" here back in 1975, when he and his partner, Bill Conkle, opened a small shop on Duval Street that quickly grew into the island's hot spot for shopping, Fast Buck Freddie's.

In 1860, a Cuban couple built the eyebrow-style home as a wedding gift for a daughter who ungraciously rejected it. When the two entrepreneurs discovered it, the house was dilapidated; they made one room livable and moved in with a hot plate and small fridge. The dust-laden hull of an old boat filled the backyard. Because of financial and time constraints, remodeling was a very slow process, but it allowed the new owners to observe the wind, rain, and path of the sun. They discovered that the house was perfectly set for two outdoor rooms, which would be shaded, would seldom feel raindrops, and could overlook two separate gardens.

Off the "meditation room" is a secret, intimate garden, its brick path warm and homey and its plantings reflecting a scrapbook of Key West remembrances. A schefflera looms thirty feet skyward, once a potted plant Tony's mother gave him for good luck when he first opened his store. Arecas are interwoven with fancy-leafed fishtail palms for a dense privacy hedge, where white, spherical, Oriental paper lanterns hang above lady palms and bird's nest anthuriums. Water trickles into a tiny pond, where goldfish swim in the

shade of travelers-trees. Philodendron vines soften the base of two memorials: a granite bench etched with the name "Bill" honors Tony's business partner and closest friend. Across the path, under bamboo palms, is a large stone engraved "Gonzo 1977-1996," a tribute to Tony's nineteen-year-old dog, the most photographed and sketched pet on the isle.

This walk of memories continues past a coverlet of leaves from a Chinese fan palm, dieffenbachia, and Tony's favorite plants, crotons. These symbols of royalty in the South Seas explode with colors from watermelon to scarlet, an incredible array of greens, yellows, tangerine, and deep-maroons. It ends in a jungly bank of giant elephant ears, white ginger, the dangling crown of a ponytail palm, and a heliconia mixture.

I sat in the outdoor "pool room," looking past the coffee table, where an orchid flowers full in multiple blooms, to a peekaboo planting pattern that gives privacy to swimmers and sunbathers. Cutouts in the pale-gray deck hold Christmas palms Tony grew from seed and corn plants so full and thick they look like palms. Licuala palms, philodendron Amazonia, and burgundy black ti plants grow as an edge garden under another paper lantern suspended within a wall of MacArthur and Christmas palms.

A flower box overflows in red pentas, and rare, white firecracker plants weep over its side. Shelves of orchids are shaded by areca palms, and a humongous croton bush, over thirty-five years old, is a hodgepodge of yellows, apricots, and oranges. Lobster claw heliconia bloom bright-red in a miniforest. An Aztec-looking crocodile doubles as a poolside bench, and a rubber gator rests on the bottom of the pool.

"My garden is Key West magic!" Tony says, and I agree.

LOCATION: **823 Eaton Street**

Flowers, Color, and Style

"For thee the wonder-working earth puts forth
   sweet flowers."

—*Lucretius*

Jerry Herman, Broadway producer of such hits as *La Cage aux Folles, Mame,* and *Hello Dolly!,* bought a decrepit pair of identical houses in the 1980s and restored them to the glistening white splendor of their nineteenth-century Classic Revival style. He sold the one on the corner and lived a low-profile life in the other. Today the owner of the house is a woman who loves color, flowers, and Key West.

Anyone walking by is as drawn to her kaleidoscopic wildflower garden as are the butterflies. They drink nectar amidst golden yellow lantanas, pink periwinkles, dark-red pentas, purple wild petunia, blue-hued plumbago, red-orange flamebush, and the lavender flowers of the golden dewdrop. A stunning Bismarck palm spreads its star-shaped fronds behind this profusion of color.

I could sense the style and grace of the woman inside as I strolled up the sidewalk to the romantic, wraparound veranda bordered in red ginger and red and peach hibiscus bushes. Inside is an extension of her garden, rooms painted the colors of her wildflowers and vases filled with the blossoms she loves to cut and bring in each morning.

In the backyard garden, over twenty orchids grace a lattice wall. A grouping of tiny vases holds nosegays of fresh flowers atop a white wicker table. A bronze bell hangs above the herb garden, where pots of basil, rosemary, and parsley grow in diffused light. At the edge of this upper deck, which overlooks the pool, is an exquisite potted bougainvillea sculpted into a tree and topped with a large globe of striking orange and pink bracts. On the corner sits a basket brimming with coral, sand dollars, starfish, helmet shells, and conch shells that were personally collected. Below, a gardenia bush spreads its fragrance.

The pool is caressed by an edge alive with bright crotons, variegated *Dracaena marginata*, and a deep-pink frangipani whose limbs are dressed in great clumps of bromeliads and Spanish moss. A row of Jerry Herman's black olive trees, native to the West Indies, stands tall and full with white orchids and staghorn ferns hanging from their zigzagging branches. A red metal sculpture by local artist John Martini stands within a thicket of huge, white birds of paradise and travelers-trees. Beneath the kitchen window, red bananas glow in their burgundy and green leaves, mingling with bolero ti plants and metal butterflies.

"I have to care for my plants like children," the owner says, smiling. "They even talk back sometimes."

LOCATION: **703 Fleming Street**

An Old Key West Feel

"That it enchants my sense."

—Shakespeare

P alm Meadow is Trip Hoffman and Alan Van Wieren's estate on the edge of Old Town. It encompasses a grand old house, built at the turn of the century and very Haitian in feel, with turrets, large windows, balconies, and a glorious wraparound verandah that looks out over a classic old Key West garden.

I reveled in that special feel of laid-back, Caribbean comfort, rocking in a white cane rocker on the porch, where tables of orchids bloom. A priceless living picture of early island life is framed within the gleaming white porch rail, with its spindles, turned columns, and simple gingerbread, all original to the house. Within its rich, green, grassy yard are two stands of edible date palms, magnificent in their sculpted multi-trunks of rich brown. A few serpentinely creep and bow along the ground while others stretch high toward the heavens. All are regally crowned with cascades of silvery blue–green feathered fronds that arc almost to the ground.

The palms, registered at Fairchild Tropical Garden for their one hundred plus years of age as well as their stature, bear tasty dates that early owners harvested, dried on the antique drying racks unearthed in the cistern house, and sold as treats to locals. Their massive root bases have created mounds, which are planted with showy bromeliads flowering in salmon-pink, yellows, and reds. Large coral rocks are artfully placed, as is a pearl-sheened jug, a replica of a Buddhist meditation piece. Scallop shells glimmer as ground cover, blanketing bare earth and roots all the way to the edge of the rich, green grass.

Washingtonian palms and old almond and autograph trees have achieved impressive heights, with a canopy that fills the sky. An unusual Jamaican teddy bear palm is gorgeous, its dark-green–ringed trunk topped with deep-sienna leaf bases irresistible to touch, as they are soft and fuzzy like teddy bears. Flower beds of blue plumbago, ginger, and bromeliads are bordered with upside-down wine bottles whose colors dance around the garden, reflecting the sun's rays.

Echoing throughout is the hypnotic sound of water from a bubbling fountain spilling into a turquoise pool. It classically sits on the grass without a deck, lined with creamy sandstone and hand-painted French tile depicting royal blue, stylized koi. This gorgeous garden-yard and unique home exemplify old, high-island class.

LOCATION: **810 Eisenhower Drive**

OF PIRATES AND PALMS

"The best treasures are yet to be found."

—Mel Fisher

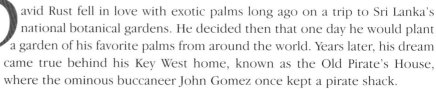

David Rust fell in love with exotic palms long ago on a trip to Sri Lanka's national botanical gardens. He decided then that one day he would plant a garden of his favorite palms from around the world. Years later, his dream came true behind his Key West home, known as the Old Pirate's House, where the ominous buccaneer John Gomez once kept a pirate shack.

David's 1848 mansion was built by Dr. Odet Phillippe, a French Navy surgeon, who, along with his family, was captured by Gomez while escaping an upper Keys Indian raid. While on board Gomez's ship, the crew contracted a "fever" but survived because of the doctor's care. The pirate rewarded Dr. Phillippe with freedom, a treasure chest, and his Key West property. But neither Gomez nor Dr. Phillippe could have dreamed of the South Seas ambiance that would become the heartbeat of the Rust garden.

Black lava rock flows as a walkway around some of the world's prettiest palms, accented by green and creamy white bossa nova bromeliads, patches of palm grass, and stands of heliconia. Golden, thick "straw" swirls around the trunk of one of the nicest Cuban old man palms on the island, planted within a stone's throw of a grand lipstick palm flaunting a multitude of bright-red trunks. This eye-catching lipstick palm was purchased from a Miami collector and is thought to be one of the largest in south Florida.

Close by is an island of black Mexican river rock, where the blue-green, striped trunk of a Haitian buccaneer palm shares space with wide-brimmed bromeliads and a *Licuala peltata,* which will grow to five feet across. The rock fades into ground covered in purple-pink Spanish shawl, where variegated Costa ginger grows on one side of a loquat tree whose branches bask in bromeliads, orchids, and air plants. At its foot is a bed of hot-pink Persian shield, a striking contrast to the dark lava rock behind it.

Close to the teal-black pool is a bed where the glamorous leaves of a Tahitian *Pelagodoxa* palm dance in the trade winds. Its silvery underleaves, glimmering as the sun shifts overhead, shade a *Licuala grandis.* Growing through the tall picket fence into the world outside is probably the oldest frangipani on the isle, its trunk incredibly thick and gnarly. Maybe Gomez enjoyed the bit of beauty and fragrance it bestowed on him, or perhaps the great tree served as a mark on a map leading to hidden treasures. Who knows what grows in a garden once owned by an infamous pirate?

LOCATION: **306 Elizabeth Street**

A FORMAL ENGLISH TROPICAL GARDEN

"Whoever wishes to attain an English style . . .
   elegant but not ostentatious. . . ."

—Samuel Adams

Three impressive Cuban royal palms, at least fifty feet tall, shade the front garden of a classy, charcoal gray Queen Anne house adorned with angled verandahs trimmed in white gingerbread. It was built in 1900 by successful wrecker George A. Roberts and originally restored years ago by President Rutherford Hayes' granddaughters, Jean and Chloe, who called it home for several years. Its street garden is a beautiful complement of red ginger, lacy pink coleus, and bromeliads with long-stemmed coral blooms and frilly ferns, all within a white picket fence. But it is the backyard that is unique in its achievement of a "formal English tropical garden," designed initially to be a white garden.

The first view is of the cluster of Alexandra palms, exquisite with all-white orchids donning their trunks, along with delicate strands of silver-white Spanish moss. Frangipani, including a rare Japanese dwarf specimen, are showered in summer's snow-white flowers, and white shell ginger blooms nearby. White wicker fills the gingerbread-trimmed gazebo, tin-roofed and fashioned after Tennessee Williams' backyard retreat over on Duncan Street. A white garden cottage is caressed by the flowers of a huge, white Hong Kong orchid tree.

Over time, subtle hints of color were added to the garden—pale-pink ginger, golden shrimp plants, and peaks of Chinese red from a stand of giant Hawaiian heliconia, whose blooms reach two feet tall. Crowns of palms weave with the drooping, leaf-clad limbs of a Brazilian olive tree, whose base is concealed by giant elephant ears and monstera leaves. Bismarck palms shimmer silver-green in unexpected starry shapes as they frame variegated bougainvillea, sculpted into a very low hedge that follows the graceful curves of the herringbone-patterned brick walkway. It leads to a seating circle of white, round-backed chairs bought at a Massachusetts antique fair.

It took a grand flair for design to create this beautiful harmony between the formal look of an English garden and the insouciance of the tropics. But then anything is possible in a Key West garden.

LOCATION: **313 William Street**

THE GARDEN OF AN ANCIENT TREE

"A man does not plant a tree for himself,
 he plants it for posterity."

—*Alexander Smith*

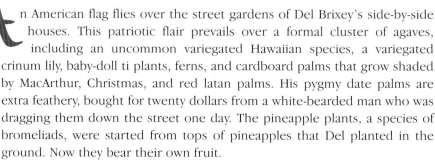

An American flag flies over the street gardens of Del Brixey's side-by-side houses. This patriotic flair prevails over a formal cluster of agaves, including an uncommon variegated Hawaiian species, a variegated crinum lily, baby-doll ti plants, ferns, and cardboard palms that grow shaded by MacArthur, Christmas, and red latan palms. His pygmy date palms are extra feathery, bought for twenty dollars from a white-bearded man who was dragging them down the street one day. The pineapple plants, a species of bromeliads, were started from tops of pineapples that Del planted in the ground. Now they bear their own fruit.

But it is the garden in back that brought the experts from Fairchild Tropical Garden to check out its masterpiece, a mammoth kapok tree they deemed to be over two hundred years old, the oldest in south Florida and in North America as well. This "grandfather" kapok is over a hundred feet tall with a 150-foot canopy, a trunk circumference of eighteen feet, and roots that look like buttresses. It bears lightning-strike scars and has withstood every hurricane that has passed over the island during its lifetime. This grand old tree continues to thrive in heartwarming surroundings, cared for by a man who values every inch of it.

Del's national treasure sits in a base of golden shrimp plants, mother-in-law tongues, gigantic bromeliads, dions, and pots of papyrus. A flat, rock waterfall, topped with cascading parrot vines, starts the flow of a stream that runs throughout the garden, ending near the kapok tree in a reflection pond adorned in bronze, arching dolphins. Another pond, at the base of the kapok, bubbles with rippling water. Around the stream and ponds are Burle Marx philodendron, royal palms, cereus cactus, rare pink jatropha, orange Geiger trees (which City Electric gave away on Arbor Day), Fiji fan palms, and liriope as ground cover. Thick, fuchsia bleeding hearts make for stunning color along trellises, which frame his beautifully restored 1850s home.

Indeed, these are exquisite surroundings, perfect for one of nature's finest and oldest masterpieces.

LOCATION: **612–614 Fleming Street**

A VERDANT PLACE

"To a green thought in a green shade."

—*Andrew Marvell*

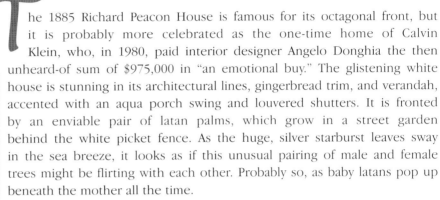

The 1885 Richard Peacon House is famous for its octagonal front, but it is probably more celebrated as the one-time home of Calvin Klein, who, in 1980, paid interior designer Angelo Donghia the then unheard-of sum of $975,000 in "an emotional buy." The glistening white house is stunning in its architectural lines, gingerbread trim, and verandah, accented with an aqua porch swing and louvered shutters. It is fronted by an enviable pair of latan palms, which grow in a street garden behind the white picket fence. As the huge, silver starburst leaves sway in the sea breeze, it looks as if this unusual pairing of male and female trees might be flirting with each other. Probably so, as baby latans pop up beneath the mother all the time.

In contrast, the garden behind the house is relaxed, informal, and mainly green. It excels in ponytail palms, which are not really palms at all but relatives of lilies and aloes. Some grow from the ground; many are potted in terra-cotta. All store water in their swollen trunks, and each has perky tops that spill over in wild heads of long, thin, wavy, lime green leaves, some over three feet long. One is particularly phenomenal, its tall, thick trunk curving into a horizontal plane, hosting many tufts of wild manes across it.

The garden is filled with true palms too, at all eye levels, from potted baby latans to short but full European fan palms and taller bamboo palms that have orange rachises bearing blue-black berries. The tall palms include queens, Alexandras, Christmases, and Cabadas. But the towering Malaysian coconut palms are the most sensational, their trunks swarming in yellow-green pothos vines. Travelers-trees spread their thick leaves like great fans jeweled in white blooms. Sun-bleached conch shells sit on cap rock that trims an old-fashioned goldfish pond shaded by papyrus. Scattered around the garden are fruit trees; little calamondin oranges add color along with key limes and pitch apples, the latter borne by autograph trees. A white, flowering henna spreads its sweet fragrance.

A pretty brick path, laid by the bricklayer who built Jayne Mansfield's heart-shaped, red hot tub in L.A., leads through the garden to the pool deck, backed by a white pergola, stunning in the morning light, which highlights a mass of pink coral vine serving as sunshade. A mirror is centered within, reflecting the greenness of it all.

This is an unpretentious garden, a place—like Key West itself—just to hang out and be yourself.

LOCATION: **712 Eaton Street**

A Personal Garden

"Heavenly blessings without number . . . ."
—Isaac Watts

O urs is a garden that's a woodland within the city," Kitty Clements said as we sat in her tin-roofed gazebo overlooking her beautiful grounds. When Kitty and her husband, Tom, bought their 1880 house as a winter home, they dreamed of creating a mini botanical garden, but the original lot was too small. To accommodate their dream, they gradually purchased the property around them, grounds occupied long ago by a cigar factory and workers' cottages. Today, the garden they have planted wraps around giant aged trees, its borders broken now and then by large, granite boulders that Kitty and Tom brought with them from a sheep pasture in Maine.

When the pool, pool house, and gazebo were designed, some of the trees stood in the way. All of them, except the two giant kapoks, were uprooted and flown through the air via cranes, replanted in new spots in the garden, and surrounded as never before in flora chosen for texture, sculpture, and botanical significance. A triangle palm stands as a one-man show, displaying its distinctive, angled, blue-green fronds at the edge of the pool, which is outlined in custom tiles in an abstract of lavenders, aquas, yellows, and pinks. Just beyond are white planters of curving seashell kalanchoe and an island, where a Madagascar olive tree, a lignum vitae, a wild ponytail palm, and a thick-leaved banana tree flourish at the foot of a looming royal palm.

Footpaths lead in different directions throughout the compound, planted with wild iris, sculpted hedges of pearl berry, willow ficus shaped into a swirling circular topiary, and a satin leaf tree (my favorite), whose under-leaves glow coppery when the wind blows. A mass of bromeliads creeps up the thorny trunk of a kapok. Beneath it, on a built-up knoll, a decorative pagoda sits amidst the exotic leaf shapes of rare palms that include the prized Seychelles stilt palm.

Around a bend, a big, terra-cotta olive jar sits within black and golden bamboo, and a Japanese tree fern grows beneath an immense octogenarian royal poinciana tree, whose massive trunk still bears the scars of a clothesline once tied too tightly. An old, wooden hot tub is chock-full of red heliconia and fragrant, creamy white clerodendrum. And then there are the fruit bearers—mangoes, carambolas, calamondin oranges, avocados, and governor's plums—which the family harvests and enjoys as celebrations of this, their personal garden.

LOCATION: **1025 Fleming Street**

A Secret Garden
of Compassion

"Love lives in gardens."

—*Caroline Giltinan*

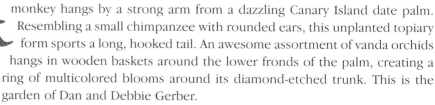

A monkey hangs by a strong arm from a dazzling Canary Island date palm. Resembling a small chimpanzee with rounded ears, this unplanted topiary form sports a long, hooked tail. An awesome assortment of vanda orchids hangs in wooden baskets around the lower fronds of the palm, creating a ring of multicolored blooms around its diamond-etched trunk. This is the garden of Dan and Debbie Gerber.

Across the antique brick walkway is an impressive clustering: eight-foot red ginger, its blooms possibly the largest on the isle, stretch into triangle palms' impressive, silvery green fronds, which spread in three directions over tall, red crown of thorns. It heralds the entry into a secret, spiritual garden, an intimate little cul-de-sac of green-ringed Cabada palms, overhanging heliconia, and gargantuan elephant ears. Pale-pink ginger entwines with lacy Ming aralea clad in orchids, protectors of a statue of Kuan Yin, a Chinese saint who, as the hearer of the cries of the world, stands as a goddess of mercy. Back at the turn of the century, Dan's grandfather fell in love with the antique, hand-carved figure on one of his trips to the Orient. Kuan Yin sailed back with him to America and held a place of honor in a grove of cedar trees at his home. Dan, who lived next door as a child, secretly visited Kuan Yin to confide his boyhood problems. She has since been handed down through the generations and continues to be sacred to Dan as she graces this secret garden designed for private thoughts.

Beyond this little sanctum, the main garden continues, wrapping around the porch of Dan's writer's studio and the eye-popping tool shed remodeled in pale-peach Greek Revival, complete with four columns and a hand-carved pineapple at its peak. The buildings are surrounded by sunny allamandas mingling with red jatropha and hibiscus, dark-colored crotons, the curvaceous trunks of spindle palms, and a trio of foxtail palms, their bushy leaves waltzing in even the slightest breeze, which carries the perfume of the ylang-ylang tree.

At one point, when Dan and Debbie thought of moving up the Keys, they put their house on the market and then visited a real estate office to look at photographs of houses for sale. Dan immediately fell in love with one of the home's gardens. The realtor smiled. "That's your own place in Key West," she said.

LOCATION: **908 Fleming Street**

Truman Annex

PRESIDENTIAL PARK

"Richness, quietness and pleasure."

—*Charles Baudelaire*

To sit in Presidential Park, open to all, is to sit within grounds where former presidents Truman, Eisenhower, Kennedy, and Carter have walked. It beautifies the main entrance to the Truman Annex, a posh, gated community built on the site of the old U.S. Naval Station, whose history dates to 1823, when it was established as headquarters for an antipiracy squadron. Major military history was made here, as the naval station served as a command post during the Spanish-American War, a submarine base during World War II, a strategic position during the Cuban missile crisis, and Harry Truman's getaway, the "Little White House."

Visitors and locals drift to this quiet spot, cooled by the canopy of the loquats, entangled with the sturdy branches of kapok trees. You can relax and daydream around the fountain, which fills the air with the mini-roar of a waterfall.

Star jasmine bloom in little white flowers, and frilly, red hibiscus mingle with yellow crotons. Deep-burgundy and bright-pink tis grow from bases of deep-yellow lantanas and red ixoras, which line brick pathways where presidents have walked.

LOCATION: **200 Front Street**

A Writer's Quiet Escape

"A thing of beauty is a joy forever."

—John Keats

I think I love Key West so much because it reminds me of my childhood years," author Judy Blume says. She has planted special reminders of her youthful spirit within her garden, like the gardenia bush, which offers her sweet perfume, pretty white flowers, and special memories every day. "Gardenias are the flowers of my youth," Judy says. "I went to every dance with a gardenia corsage."

Her hibiscus bushes are equally as precious. "In the late forties, when I lived in Miami," she says, "I plucked one hibiscus every day on the way to school, put it behind my ear and played like I was Esther Williams. I love my hibiscus, especially the peachy ones. They allow me to be ten years old again. But I can't stand it that you only get the beautiful bloom for one day and then it is gone.

"I also love to fill the basket on my bike with orchids and ride home from the plant shop at the M.A.R.C. House (Monroe County Association for Retarded Citizens). You can do that here in Key West. Buy them today and lovingly care for them while they are blooming. Then I attach them to my palm trees for their next blooming."

Her verandah, which overlooks the pool, is clad in these orchids in every color imaginable. Some sit atop gorgeous tables, once display tables at Fast Buck Freddie's. Others sit on the floor beside pots of another one of her favorites, areca palms, butterfly-graceful in their long, arching, feathery fronds.

A bit of Key West whimsy prevails in "La Fontana di Lulu," a hand-carved figurehead that once stood sentry at the entrance to the island's nautical antique store before Judy and her husband, George, brought her home. George attached Lulu to a fountain wall, where water spills from two antique, brass candlesticks into a pond below. The couple dress Lulu for "modesty reasons" in swimsuit tops, cool shades, hats, and colorful beads collected at Fantasy Fest, the island's Halloween celebration. She watches over the garden, whose pool-length wall is a lattice attached to a mirror, reflecting a container collection that holds plants from asparagus ferns to big, red-leafed bananas. The garden continues hugging the patio in bright-yellow thryallis, fuchsia bleeding hearts, the huge leaves of travelers-trees, and more arecas, creating a poolside paradise that blocks out the world.

On the other side of the house is Judy's little secret garden. It's always "a surprise and delight" for her to walk out of her writing room and into this coveted sanctuary. It blends the Southern look of Savannah—a black, wrought-iron table and chairs for two on a coral red, antique brick patio—with the tropical look of red ginger and ti plants the color of warm, red wine. Walking in this sanctuary brings Judy the joy of discovering the new blooms of all the orchids she has tied to a privacy hedge of dense palms. The only thing she loves more is spending an evening with George on the verandah, dining by candlelight with the arecas swaying in the sea breeze. A sliver of a moon shines against the midnight blue sky, and the garden is filled with the sweet scent of the gardenias of her youth.

LULU'S WEBSITE: www.panix.com/~gcooper/lulu.html

THE CAPTAIN
AND HIS ROSES

"Gather the roses of life today."

—*Pierre de Ronsard*

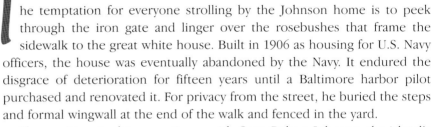

The temptation for everyone strolling by the Johnson home is to peek through the iron gate and linger over the rosebushes that frame the sidewalk to the great white house. Built in 1906 as housing for U.S. Navy officers, the house was eventually abandoned by the Navy. It endured the disgrace of deterioration for fifteen years until a Baltimore harbor pilot purchased and renovated it. For privacy from the street, he buried the steps and formal wingwall at the end of the walk and fenced in the yard.

The maritime tradition continues with Capt. Robert Johnson, the island's longest-standing working harbor pilot, who guides cruise ships safely into port. Robert and his wife, Roberta, not to be hemmed in anywhere, opened the gateway to the street, unearthed the traditional wingwalls and stairs, and reconnected them to the sidewalk. Roses, specially ordered for the tropical climate, now border the walkway, magnificent in deep, velvety crimsons, hot-pinks, rich corals, sunny yellows, pale pinks, angelic white, and even dusky blue. They well over in buds and huge, open blossoms all year long. It's the perfect place to stop and smell our national flower.

This garden is an exemplary blend of tropical and traditional. The rich, grassy areas, where grandchildren play, stretch between thick mounds of impatiens—over two hundred of them in a riot of colors—interspersed with elephant ears. Shade is offered by a triangle palm, queen palms, and a dramatic old sea grape tree covered with circular leaves and bunches of ripe, purple sea grapes, which make great jelly.

A calamondin orange tree, a hybrid of the Mandarin orange and kumquat, provides the sweet pulp and rind for Roberta's old island treat, calamondin cake. The captain and his wife pick key limes right off their tree to squeeze into their special Bloody Marys, which they sip as they sit on their porch looking out over their garden. They walk their garden most evenings just to admire the flowers, lingering at the fence and looking back from the same vantage point as the people who peep through the gate. They like to talk to passersby about their flowers, then return via the "roseway," smelling the fragrances, noting which are blooming, and always cutting roses to grace their dining room table.

This garden exudes a tranquil, safe, and stable feel. It's the kind we all loved as children and all seek as adults.

LOCATION: **324 Whitehead Street**

A Garden Fronts the Sea

"The trees seem to march seaward still."

—S. O. Jewett

Wedding-white stephanotis softens the long, white picket fence of one of the largest estates on the island. The fence is low enough for everyone passing by to view the extensive gardens beyond, which inspire artists to set up easels on the sidewalk and paint the day away.

Brilliant red Turks caps, which look like sleeping hibiscus, bloom in front of a stand of banana trees. The flower spikes of orchids stretch from the trees they cling to toward the gate, which opens onto a regal row of queen palms creatively interspersed with silver thatch palms, still immature yet so full they resemble glittery bushes. The palm walkway leads to the splendor of the white mansion, where former president Dwight Eisenhower and his wife, Mamie, once stayed. It was built in 1918 as surgeons' quarters for the naval hospital next door but later became home to a number of naval base commanders.

From here, crotons, neon-bright in the sunshine, shade lady palms and gingers of all colors, which follow the contours of the garden path to the back of the house, which overlooks the waters of the harbor. Blue herons and white egrets often fly in and rest poolside amidst the deep-pinks of desert rose and magnificent bottle palms.

Pinwheel jasmine, with its tiny yellow centers, surrounds bottle palms and dark-green dions. The ground slopes up a mound to a beautiful oil palm, ponytail palms, and corn plants amidst the maroon undersides of big, red banana leaves. Palm grass grows beneath colossal screw pines, possibly the most impressive on the island, looming in woven patterns of green, whirling leaves. Nearby, a sitting area is graced with sophisticated white furniture, coconut palms, and a little forest of red heliconia.

The wind really whispers here through the collection of towering palms— three triangle palms; a Canary Island date, whose trunk is filled with ferns; and gigantic cardboard palms. Bismarck and fishtail palms watch over a bed of golden shrimp plants. Travelers-trees, a gorgeous *Copernicia berteroana* (native to the Dominican Republic), a gebang palm, foxtails, and fan palms make an exotic and exciting background for the three triangles of sixty-foot royal palms that tower over the fence out front.

"We are never in a hurry to leave," the owners said as we walked the garden. "And we are always in a hurry to get back."

LOCATION: **51 Front Street**

PEACE OF PARADISE GARDEN

"Beauty is that which attracts your soul."

—*Kahlil Gibran*

The rest of the world feels far removed within the elegance of a garden called "Peace of Paradise." It is a South Seas plantation dipped in the subtle, chocolatey scent of a pink floss silk tree, its trunk covered in pink-hued "barnacles" tipped with barbs. The gentle sound of water flows from the foundation of an outdoor "living room" into the teal-black pool below.

A colossal Puerto Rican hat palm reaches fifty feet into the air, towering over a zigzagging line of Washingtonian palms, their trunks dressed in layers of dried, golden tan petticoats. The red, fuzzy fingers of chenille plants dance in the wind beside the unflappable red crown of thorns. Three stout trunks of a large ponytail palm are topped with a mane of streaming leaves and a statue of St. Francis of Assisi stands beneath silver saw palmetto. Coconuts ripen within the crown of palms, and tiki gods, hand-carved from tree trunks, frame a bend in the walkway, where impatiens in vivid colors grow within deep grooves of coral rock. A statue of a little boy holding a conch shell sits surrounded by exotic philodendron.

The king of the garden is a mammoth Bismarck palm, probably the largest and showiest on the isle, topped with awesome, silvery green leaves, some bent in the middle, looking like great plumed birds. It sits poolside in a cutout of Black Magic ti plants and a wonderful duo of pachypodiums, which are relatives of lilies. A pair of sweet little angels sits on the edge of the pool, looking as if they are sharing miracles.

The outdoor room is open on all sides, presenting many different views of this gorgeous, extensive garden, where a meditative aura reigns. The room's supporting white columns are topped with carved conch shells, and its cathedral ceiling is painted sky blue. It is furnished with dark-green wicker and pots of areca palms and dracaenas adorn each corner. All is shaded from the noonday sun by a great stand of travelers-trees and a wall of heliconia.

A stroll beyond the main garden is also wonder-filled: a wide-trunked Canary Island date palm; stands of huge, red bananas whose trunks glow red when the sun hits them; and a surprise entryway into a wildflower garden filled with deep- and pastel-pink pentas, golden dewdrops, milkweed, and papaya trees heavily laden with tropical fruit.

This garden is where South Seas dreams come true.

LOCATION: **Truman Annex**

100

A COLLECTOR'S GARDEN

"Cherish that which is within you . . . "

—*Chuang-tzu*

I met the Timyans on their back porch, which overlooks their garden. We sat at a table set in yellow and orange, with a large vase of cut flowers at its center. Great candleholders and pots of orchids with tiny blooms were scattered about. Pat is a woman who loves her collection of treasures, many of which adorn her garden.

"I walk my garden a lot," she said, "looking for places to put my ornaments."

She showed me how she attached a turquoise Aztec mask to a sabal palm and how whelk shells are lodged within the leaf bases of other palms. A small bust sits within a concrete picture frame on a mound of mulch, while another, larger bust, a Nero look-alike, is bejeweled in beaded necklaces as it sits amidst large monstera leaves at pool's edge. Little mirrors hang from tree trunks, reflecting sunlight and views of the garden.

Six tall, metal sculptures made by local sculptor John Martini flow from inside the house out through the garden. They add rustic color, plus Martini's unique combination of classical and primitive inspiration to this garden, which is bathed in a tropical mix that really starts in the front yard, distinguishing it from its neighbors.

The formalized stairway off the entrance is flanked by Florida thatch palms, orange-red ixoras, pentas, and golden dewdrops. They blend into privacy walls of Montgomery and queen palms and an uncommon frangipani that blooms year-round. Bougainvillea spills over the white picket fence.

Along the brick path that surrounds the house is a dense planting of silver buttonwood trees, palmettos, royals, paurotis, latan, and bamboo palms. In their shade are classy clusters of lady and European fan palms. They eventually curve around the custom pool, mystical in its black glow, designed to give as much space as possible to the garden.

Fresh herbs such as rosemary and oregano grow off the back porch, which overlooks patches of blue daze, pink pentas, purple wild petunias, and peach-yellow crossandras. A tall, purple-pink clerodendrum blooms in winter, as do red and peach hibiscus. A unique collection of terra-cotta pots, bought at roadside stands, is scattered about.

The indoor/outdoor shower, screened by bamboo, carries on the island tradition of backyard bathing *en plein air.*

LOCATION: **52 Front Street**

A Garden of Romance

"Retreating, to the breath
 Of the night-wind . . ."

—Russell H. Conwell

The home and gardens of John and Jamie Hallick are a picture of island elegance. The coppery branches of red-barked gumbo limbo trees unite over the dark-green gateway. Just steps beyond, the calming sounds of water flow down a four-tier fountain, which enhances the formality of the two-story estate, built in 1941 as quarters for naval officers. The garden behind the house is a sophisticated seductress.

The siren's song of the garden is its waterfall, a dramatic mosaic depicting the sun, moon, and sky. Little pieces of Venetian glass sparkle like jewels within the surrounding brightly colored ceramic tiles. A delicate sheet of water spills over the Mexican Tikul stone ledge, creating the sound of a gentle tropical rain or, with the flip of a switch, the roar of nature's great falls. It flows into a lagoon-shaped pool. Stunning in daylight, it is drop-dead gorgeous at night.

Rich clusters of cat palms frame the fountain, with towering coconut palms, silver buttonwoods, Bismarck palms, ginger, and angel's trumpets, all taking on a special aura as they are reflected in the water. A secret path leads to a miniature cul-de-sac, where a Jacuzzi is steeped in the privacy of draping heliconia, dappled crotons, and looming fishtail and coconut palms trimmed to allow a "skylight," through which stars show.

The addictive scent used in Chanel No. 5 floats on the sea breeze, released from the blossoms of the ylang-ylang tree. Jamie encloses them in lettersshe writes. It's a special way to share the essence of her Key West garden with loved ones up North.

LOCATION: **328 Whitehead Street**

A Mermaid Bathed in Palms

"I fetched my sea-born treasure home . . ."

—*Ralph Waldo Emerson*

A temptress of the surrounding sea is the star in a garden just beyond the gate of a white picket fence. A mermaid, golden bronze and glowing as the sun's rays catch her, is posed. One arm reaches up, the gaze of her eyes following it. Her long, dark hair caresses her shoulders. She appears to be swimming skyward from the great depths of the sea.

She is pure "island," standing six feet tall in a little side garden, where the rush of water is heard from beyond. Encircling her are the ringed trunks of Christmas palms and bushy-fronded foxtail palms. Huge, flat rocks scatter their rusty colors amidst the green, some supporting long-leafed bromeliads, others sitting beside clusters of Xanadu, blue plumbago, and yellow thryallis. Deep-burgundy ti plants sit beside taller, wispier, pink-leafed, tri-color dracaenas. The silver-white leaves of buttonwoods mingle with pink hibiscus as they grow over the fence.

This mermaid is queen of a setting most only dream of.

LOCATION: **66 Front Street**

Gardens out of Town

A WANDERING WONDERLAND

"And dreaming eyes of wonder!"

—*Lewis Carroll*

When artist John Kiraly opened his front door, he welcomed me into the breathtaking entry to his garden. Like his famous canvasses, it is a vision of tropical escape I think Lewis Carroll would have loved to travel. Thick veils of long pothos philodendron vines dangle from roof to ground near the first of many waterfalls. Miniature rolling hills, covered with fluffy zoysiagrass, hold hidden treasures in their "valleys," such as the stark, white sculpture of a man's head with piercing eyes. Nearby are an Italian table and chairs carved in the delicate curves of giant mushrooms.

A man who loves to shape plants, John sculpts everything in circles, ovals, and crescent moons. A Norfolk pine has taken on the fantasy-like form of a wide umbrella whose tips curve upward, and nearby a gumbo limbo's red trunk is enshrouded in a swirl of lavender orchids.

John built the bricked water fountain which inspired his painting entitled *Key West Garden*. Along the path a pergola drips bougainvillea, a bronze Buddha sits at pond's edge, and a Victorian corner offers wind chimes and an ornate loveseat caressed by torch ginger, his favorite flower. An agave collection, accented in sculptures, is the centerpiece of his swimming pool.

"I feel a part of me is expressed one way on canvas," John said, "and another way in the garden. But I see the paintings in the garden . . . and the garden in the paintings."

Both are true works of art.

LOCATION: **3820 Eagle Avenue**

A Caribbean Corner

"All that in this delightful garden grows,
Should happy be . . ."

—*Edmund Spenser*

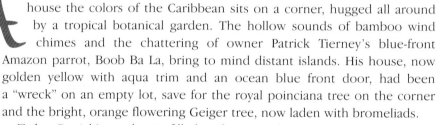

A house the colors of the Caribbean sits on a corner, hugged all around by a tropical botanical garden. The hollow sounds of bamboo wind chimes and the chattering of owner Patrick Tierney's blue-front Amazon parrot, Boob Ba La, bring to mind distant islands. His house, now golden yellow with aqua trim and an ocean blue front door, had been a "wreck" on an empty lot, save for the royal poinciana tree on the corner and the bright, orange flowering Geiger tree, now laden with bromeliads.

Today, Patrick's garden is filled with rare palms along with varieties of bananas, heliconia, and elephant ears. "It's not a garden I would plan for someone else," says Patrick, a landscape artist. "This is more like my outpost, a research station where I experiment with plants from different parts of the world."

My favorite palm is the impressive *Sabal yapa dominicalis,* native to Guyana, with its large, blue-green, circular leaves which grow into a thirty-foot span before the tree shows a trunk at age ten. Another beauty is the Sagisi palm, native to the rainforests of the South Pacific. There are also great specimens of buccaneers, a triangle palm, and a tall, lofty Puerto Rican thatch palm. A thick-trunked ponytail palm is tucked into a mini-forest of heliconia, whose long, red bracts are remarkable within all the greenery. Patrick grew the stunning, pleated-leafed Fiji fan palm from seed collected on the northern rim of Oahu.

Dinosaurs would have a feast here on the rows of dions, descendants of ancient plants. The *Philodendron rubioso* is unique in its maroon-hued emerging leaves. Wavy, thorn-studded trunks of pachypodiums grow beside butter-yellow crotons, rosettes of spineless agave, aloes, bromeliads, and a Janet Craig Compacta, a gorgeous hybrid of a dracaena.

All types of dracaenas grow in a large bed in front of a woven bamboo fence topped with passion vines bearing both fruit and flowers. Patrick's rare alocasia collection grows below, with stunning leaves that appear to have been splattered with creamy white paint. Across the walk is the largest of banana trees, with its red-hued trunk and deep-red stalks of bananas. An uncommon species of frangipani blooms white all year long.

Colorful buoys, washed in from the sea, hang from the rafters of a Caribbean-colored pergola, where Patrick pots and nurtures plants. It sits beside a tin-roofed tool shed, painted the colors of the rainbow, where bougainvillea and a desert rose bloom. Boob Ba La chatters. The wind ruffles the heliconia leaves, and the essence of frangipani filles the air. Ah! How a garden enhances life!

LOCATION: **2803 Seidenberg Avenue**

A Tribute to Roberto Burle Marx

"Fond memory brings the light of other days around me."

—Thomas Moore

’m a restless sensualist who loves to see things grow," award-winning landscape architect Raymond Jungles says. Nowhere is that more evident than at his own home. The small estate of Raymond and his wife, Debra Yates, has been in Debra's family for sixty years, so theirs is a garden of old island trees, rare species, and bold, colorful walls. It is Raymond's experimental laboratory, where the spirit of his mentor, legendary Brazilian artist and landscape architect Roberto Burle Marx, is alive.

Memories of enjoying cocktails with his mother-in-law in the openness of his home's front porch influenced Raymond to keep the front exposed as a "public" garden. It has a look all its own, with an aging tropical almond tree, its lower branches covered with bromeliads, standing out against a backdrop of bright walls in Barragan red, yellow-orange, lavender, and olive green. Staghorn ferns thrive in the crooks of a sapodilla tree, and an old fiddle leaf grows with Washingtonians, one of which was planted long ago by Raymond's father-in-law. Anthuriums and licuala palms grow in a carpet of shaggy zoysiagrass; a swollen, ring-trunked Haitian wine palm neighbors a rare South African cycad. The bright lipstick palm sits behind hot-pink bromeliads; a rare, shooting-star clerodendrum (my favorite), a

prize from a trip to Monte Verde, Costa Rica, is magnificent with its five-pointed star "etched" on each white flower. And the essences of ylang-ylang, bay rum, and allspice trees drift throughout.

Near the louvered door to a separate, private garden is a watermelon-colored croton, stunning against the lavender wall; the top of a huge stand of black bamboo towers over another, coral-colored wall. The door opens onto a very rare, fernlike cycad; an uncommon, variegated lady palm; carpentaria palms, planted long ago when they were still considered rare; and a Christmas palm, which is Raymond's orchid holder.

Orange-red glory bowers spread color beside a rare *Chamaedorea metallica,* which bears bright-orange seeds and a metallic sheen. A rare, prehistoric-looking Sansevieria, which Raymond brought from the home of Burle Marx, is a plant he loves for its fragrance. And then there is Raymond's "baby," his colossal South American oil palm, with its thirty-foot fronds and gigantic leaf bases. A stainless steel bench reflects the sun and the dancing shadows of the surrounding palms.

The pool garden is a tribute to both unusual palms and the memory of Roberto Burle Marx, whose large, ceramic mural—created in aqua, black, gray, and white—hangs on a fountain wall topped with double-yellow allamandas and true Philippine dogwood weeping with peach-pink flowers. Rare palms frame the area, including the magnificent Satake palm from the Ryukyu Islands, a swollen silver thatch, with its finely spun, golden, woven thatch curling and swirling around its trunk, and a gorgeous specimen of a buccaneer palm, the rarest of Florida natives.

Raymond Jungles' garden is a "living work of art." His mentor, Roberto Burle Marx, would be proud of it.

LOCATION: **Casa Marina area**

TRANQUILITY FROM THE ORIENT

"My soul's calm retreat
Which none disturb!"

—Henry Vaughan

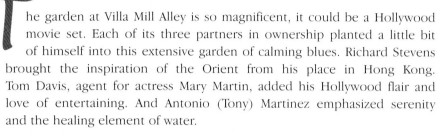

The garden at Villa Mill Alley is so magnificent, it could be a Hollywood movie set. Each of its three partners in ownership planted a little bit of himself into this extensive garden of calming blues. Richard Stevens brought the inspiration of the Orient from his place in Hong Kong. Tom Davis, agent for actress Mary Martin, added his Hollywood flair and love of entertaining. And Antonio (Tony) Martinez emphasized serenity and the healing element of water.

Three fountains lend their sounds of flowing water to the main garden all the way to the base of the Moon Gate, a circular cutout trimmed in cobalt blue that, according to Chinese legend, is the opening to a better life. It frames the full, draping leaves of an aborea, the largest of dracaenas. A Fu dog is positioned on either side of the gate as protection: a male stands on the world, and a female is poised on a baby.

A bed of yellow-orange ixoras, golden shrimp plants, and bright crotons beautifies the "cocktail area," its table surrounded with Chinese garden seats fashioned from porcelain stoneware with ornate, blue motifs.

Water trickles into a pond where large koi swim within the safety of several varieties of water plants: hyacinth, cabbage, and lilies. Canna lilies, papyrus, and horsetails also grow from the depths of the water. A pair of bronze cranes stands within the innocence of bright moss roses, red and yellow-green coleus, red powderpuffs, and a gorgeous triangle palm, one of three within the garden.

A cobalt blue bridge, another Oriental garden feature, crosses the stream that flows from the pond to a pagoda-style pergola, where Tony and I sat, taking time to enjoy the details of the garden—statues of elephants and frogs, Chinese ginger jars, a cluster of black bamboo, a fake yet real-looking snake wrapped around a tree trunk, lanterns whose flames light the garden by night, and Oriental gingerbread and screens, which grace the houses of the compound.

Peace lilies line one side of a walkway; bromeliads grow in the shadows of coconut palms, on whose trunks staghorn ferns and orchids flourish. The walkway ends in an open-air dining pagoda, where Tom hosted his famous dinner parties before he passed on. He started the garden and filled it with mature plants that he could enjoy in their full splendor.

"This garden is very special," Tony says. "It gave Tom a reason to get up each day."

LOCATION: **Mill Alley**

A Water Garden Gallery, Barbados-Style

"For 'tis my outward soul."

—*John Donne*

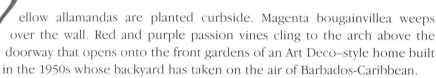

Yellow allamandas are planted curbside. Magenta bougainvillea weeps over the wall. Red and purple passion vines cling to the arch above the doorway that opens onto the front gardens of an Art Deco–style home built in the 1950s whose backyard has taken on the air of Barbados-Caribbean.

For the owners of this house, water was the key. They had lived their lives oceanside in St. Thomas, Virgin Islands, before moving to Key West. And they wanted a garden without work, just something lush and green. So they designed a water garden—a cool, clear pond where water flows on each side, down the staggered steps and crevices of layered Tennessee stone, which resounds with the calmness of a gentle rain.

The rustic stone is carried into the patio, where it covers a wall whose '50s-style windows are camouflaged with wooden shutters stained the color of teak on a fine yacht. The stone-and-wood combination is pure Barbados, reminiscent of its old plantation days, and sets the feel of the garden. Its dense, verdant background is a mixture of all the common palms, a rubber tree, song of India, and palm grass.

One side of the pond hosts a great grouping of terra-cotta pottery, some tilted on their sides, some broken. A basket of coconuts—each painted either bronze, gold, silver, or green—serves as an islandy, decorative piece. Opposite is a stone sculpture done by a local artist who has been inspired by the history of Southwest American Indians. It all blends perfectly with the patio's roof, curvaceous in Art Deco style. Its weight-bearing columns are painted to resemble bamboo; its ceiling is a lovely lavender, with a domed skylight beaming sunlight onto a collection of antique oil cans sitting on an old wooden chest. A John Martini metal sculpture stands beside it. The sunny part of the patio is furnished in iron or steel furniture, which gives the sense of mass and weight the owners love. Metal sculptures of roosters and mocko jumbies, symbols of the Caribbean, are scattered about, gorgeous original works by the lady of the house, who loves creating in metal.

This, indeed, is a lot more than a water garden. It is a tropical gallery that expresses the carefree spirit of its owners.

LOCATION: **Flagler Avenue**

THE GLAMOUR OF OLD KEY WEST

*"Trees and stones will teach us that
which you can never learn from the masters."*

—St. Bernard

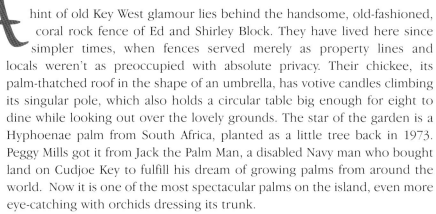

A hint of old Key West glamour lies behind the handsome, old-fashioned, coral rock fence of Ed and Shirley Block. They have lived here since simpler times, when fences served merely as property lines and locals weren't as preoccupied with absolute privacy. Their chickee, its palm-thatched roof in the shape of an umbrella, has votive candles climbing its singular pole, which also holds a circular table big enough for eight to dine while looking out over the lovely grounds. The star of the garden is a Hyphoenae palm from South Africa, planted as a little tree back in 1973. Peggy Mills got it from Jack the Palm Man, a disabled Navy man who bought land on Cudjoe Key to fulfill his dream of growing palms from around the world. Now it is one of the most spectacular palms on the island, even more eye-catching with orchids dressing its trunk.

Another gem is a large lignum vitae tree, estimated to be over a century old. It shades part of the porch in a sea of springtime flowers similar to little African violets. The sight is so memorable, the owners have been encouraged to celebrate it with an annual lignum vitae party. And that stone wall that serves as background to a palm collection? It was built from the coral taken out of the ground when the swimming pool was dug. Also from the excavation came voodoo dolls from the days when the land was a hardwood hammock. The workers ran off the job when they saw them and refused to return. A Cuban man took the dolls away, saying he would make sure they would be put where they belonged. The workers came back and the pool was finished.

Unusual terra-cotta pots are scattered around the pool, and the porches are decorated with yellow ixoras, peace lilies, Hawaiian lilies, and blue plumbago, as well as an old man palm and *Licuala*, both *splendida* and *grandis*. All is accentuated with a mass of magenta bougainvillea growing behind two bronze cranes, which stand as guardians of this glamorous garden.

LOCATION: **1300 Tropical Street**

STREAMS OF COLOR, SOUNDS OF RAIN

"World, you are beautifully dressed."

—*Matthew Brown*

The element of water reigns in this masculine garden. When its owner moved here more than fifteen years ago, he transformed the typical, bright-blue swimming pool into a "lagoon," with naturally curved edges of coral stone, its bottom painted an infinite black. Then he purchased his neighbor's property, whose pool was within a few feet of his lagoon but was elevated two feet. So he recreated the lagoon look and ingeniously connected both pools with a three-tiered waterfall of black river rock, which enriches the air with the hypnotic sound of tumbling water. The waters reflect a dreamy picture of the surrounding gardens, which couldn't be more beautiful.

Each side of the original pool is planted in intimate groupings, the colors laid out as if by an artist. The deep pinks of ti plants and the lemon-lime of the leaves of the song of India are mingled with brilliant impatiens and the scarlet crown of thorns, which follow the contours of the coral rock. Emerald and purple queens, as well as exotic philodendron vines, peek out from behind the flowers. A native white Geiger tree is covered with delicate, snow-white flowers close to a rubber tree, which stretches above crinum lilies and lady palms. Red hibiscus, sculpted into trees, bloom everywhere, along with peace lilies.

Wooden loveseats and chairs are poised for different views of the garden on a deck of swirling, earth-tone Tennessee Apple Orchard stone. The deck melts into an area shaded from the sun by a cathedral ceiling, which joins the two houses of the adjoining yards and takes on a Mediterranean flair from the huge terra-cotta oil jugs from Greece and Morocco. On the outer wall of the second house is another water design, an exquisite fountain of Chinese blue-green tile that changes hue with the sun's rays. Its summer-rain chorus adds to this harmonious setting, where the owner works each day.

"I like my garden," the owner says. "When I'm on the telephone out here, people up north always ask if it's raining. I say, 'No, it's just the waterfalls in my garden.' "

LOCATION: **Casa Marina area**

FOUNTAINS AND FRAGRANCE

"Sounds and sweet airs, that give delight . . . ."

—Shakespeare

The Dunn family wanted a garden that combined romance, fragrance, and lots of color. They got it. A huge Cuban laurel tree marks the *Jetsons*-style entrance to their domain. Pale-chartreuse columns and a green-washed louver door blend into the side privacy wall, where show-stopping, papery-pink flowers drape over a sinuous periwinkle wall. The wall's final graceful curve melds into a straight-lined teal wall dripping with magenta bougainvillea topped with Cherries Jubilee allamandas. Simpson stopper trees grow along the public sidewalk, bathed in a ground cover of yellow kalanchoe.

The privacy wall envelops a "refined" 1950s Art Deco–style house built by Charlie Toppino. The story goes that there is a home just like it in the hills outside Havana, Cuba, where the American ambassador lived. Toppino saw it in the late '40s, searched for its architect, and built its twin here

The green-washed door opens onto a Zen-like path of black Mexican river rock that leads past two companion, abstract, ceramic fountain murals in royal blue, red, black, and green. Each is surrounded by a mix of Confederate jasmine and Cabada palms, with an extremely rare chartreuse alocasia outshining all else.

Bismarck palms, black ironwood, and ylang-ylang trees grow near a cluster of wispy-leafed, black bamboo. Orchids of all sizes and colors dress many of the trees. The poolside loggia has a fun, futuristic look, with chartreuse columns, cut-out ceiling, and whirring, silver ceiling fans. The furniture is silver too, prizes from second-hand stores and junk shops in their old Venice Beach, California, neighborhood. The area is filled with palms accented by very rare chamaedoreas, whose new fronds pop out a deep dark-red before turning dark-green.

Another mural/fountain, topped with dwarf silver palmettos, spills into the pool, surrounded by Spanish Shawl that covers the bases of Simpson stoppers, native to Florida hammocks. In the shade, rare gold and black Sansevieria is stunning in its base of black beach rocks.

A secret little orchard is tended by Steve and Dale, who harvest varieties of bananas and oranges. The old mango tree is covered with fruit, artistically dangling on the ends of cords in shades of purple, red, yellow, and green. It just doesn't get any more tropical than this.

LOCATION: **Casa Marina area**

A MEDITATIVE SETTING

"Meditation and waters are wedded forever."

—*Herman Melville*

When Hurricane Georges ripped though the yard of Karen Harte, toppling her old trees, she took it as a sign to start anew with a garden that was a true reflection of her personality and philosophy. It is magnificently meditative in every sense of the word. A secret Buddha sits within a circle of black bamboo. Burmese gongs hang from coconut palms. A coral-stone stairway, framed with blue plumbago, reddish black bromeliads, and bird's nest anthuriums, lead up a mound to where two stone elephants sit at the entrance to a luxurious, open-air chickee. The elephants were carved from stone that came from a wall in the town where Ghandi was born.

In the chickee, it is about ten degrees cooler than in the sunny air just steps away. I sat on a settee made of an antique Indonesian loom, where I breathed in the sensuous aroma of straw still lingering from the dried palm fronds Guatamalan artisans had woven into its thatched roof. Beyond a bed of railroad ferns and magenta ti plants, water cascades down three tiers of coral fashioned into a natural streambed. The mood is contemplative as the water flows past large chunks of pyrite, amethyst, and rose quartz gemstones shimmering in the sun and on into a black-bottom pond. It is a Jacuzzi in disguise, shaded by huge elephant ears and monstera leaves and surrounded by bromeliads and Spanish shawl.

Another picture of tranquillity is a gleaming, bronze Buddha seated in lotus posture, centered in a mass planting on the back wall of a rectangular swimming pool. On each side of Siddhartha are large, female latan palms amidst a mass of Burle Marx philodendron. Water gently bubbles up and spills over unpolished marble tiles into the pool. A third Buddha blesses the garden, seated between pool's edge and the porch of the bright-yellow and hot-pink–trimmed guest house. Hand-painted mirrors, Karen's original artwork, hang on all the outside walls of the main house and guest cottage, reflecting every angle of the garden that has captured the essence of Karen Harte's soul.

LOCATION: **716 Seminary Street**

122

A Garden Linked to Tennessee Williams

". . . a bit of fun and relaxation . . . ."

—Herodotus

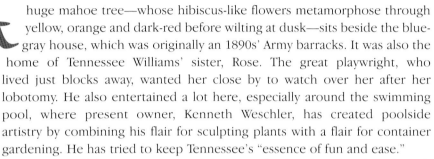

A huge mahoe tree—whose hibiscus-like flowers metamorphose through yellow, orange and dark-red before wilting at dusk—sits beside the blue-gray house, which was originally an 1890s' Army barracks. It was also the home of Tennessee Williams' sister, Rose. The great playwright, who lived just blocks away, wanted her close by to watch over her after her lobotomy. He also entertained a lot here, especially around the swimming pool, where present owner, Kenneth Weschler, has created poolside artistry by combining his flair for sculpting plants with a flair for container gardening. He has tried to keep Tennessee's "essence of fun and ease."

As I entered the gate to the pool deck, I walked under a low, bare branch of the mahoe shaped into an archway wrapped in twinkle lights. A ghost orchid hangs in its crook, flowering fragile white. The mahoe also hosts a wind chime that plays beach music as the air swings the antique, sea-glass bottle tops suspended from driftwood.

A replica of a 1920s' Art Nouveau urn sits at the head of the pool, with a bonsai split-leafed philodendron growing out the top, its abstract roots crawling down its sides. White ornamental pots run the length of the pool, filled with cheerful plants such as the red-flowered jatropha, a corkscrew-trunked pink hibiscus with a cherub at its feet, and the powderpuff, with its cherry red, airy blooms. Visitors always grin at the row of five smiling rubber duckies fronting a fence of fuschia pandorea vines.

An amazingly large yellow croton is rooted in another pot, and a bonsai fiddle-leaf fig, which gets its roots pruned annually, thrives in a pot so small it seems miraculous that the plant's leaves are normal size. A wispy-fronded thurston palm, probably the tallest on the island, grows from the ground, watered by the outdoor shower. It is surrounded by scheffleras sculpted to look like lollipops.

Two steps down off the pool deck is a small, grassy, island-style area where two old Jamaican Tall coconut palms bear hooks, upon which either a hammock swings or stalks of bananas are hung to ripen. They're surrounded by the variegated gingers Ken loves. Two little pink flamingoes, so old they're made of concrete, lend a bit of an old Florida look to this garden mainly sown in little pots of earth.

LOCATION: **915 Von Phister Street**

INDEX